I0756732

THE WAR OF DESTINY

TRIGGERS OF INSURGENT EVOLUTION

DOMINIC UKELO

authorHOUSE®

AuthorHouse™ UK
1663 Liberty Drive
Bloomington, IN 47403 USA
www.authorhouse.co.uk
Phone: 0800.197.4150

Published by AuthorHouse 05/15/2019

ISBN: 978-1-7283-8826-7 (sc)
ISBN: 978-1-7283-8827-4 (hc)
ISBN: 978-1-7283-8825-0 (e)

CONTENTS

Part 4

ACKNOWLEDGEMENTS

It has seemed to me embarrassing that much of the Western Bahr el Ghazal (WBG) region history, in the Republic of South Sudan (RSS), was written by noncitizens of the region. Instead of the sons and daughters of the WBG region being the main references of their own history, the foreigners were taking this privilege to tell the world about what happened there.

As somebody who was born in the WBG region, Wau City, I am very capable of bringing to the readers, through this book, my Western academic experiences and the real experiences of these historical events. Studying and working in Western countries gave me an opportunity to go through experiences and acquire knowledge about how to prevent triggers of ethnic conflict, perhaps by putting in place a system of governance that suits the needs of those of different backgrounds and ethnic groups.

Though I am not the first to write about the ethnic conflicts in the country, this book is the best one to describe the historical events that caused the ethnic conflicts, the civil war, and the recommendations for the way forward for the Republic of South Sudan. However, it was not easy to combine and compare significant historical information in order to build this book.

First, thanks are owed to the political and military leaders of the WBG region for giving me both the privilege and information in order to build this study. As these historical events were emerging in the past, each leader documented these events. Most of these leaders then gave me their own notices, which became the original sources of this book.

Second, thanks go to the people of WBG, especially to those with whom I spoke in the form of interviews. The information I acquired from both the leaders and the people of the region was genuine and led me to correct some secondary sources that I found.

The sixty-four different ethnic groups in the Republic of South Sudan can live together in peace and harmony, if the government treated its citizens equally and introduced a system of governance that encourages the people in the country to live together as one nation in peace. The members of government who commit tribalism, are corrupt, and violate the rights of other communities are mostly Jieng elites. But a large number of ordinary Jieng civilians were kind enough to share their thoughts on how different ethnic groups in the country can live together. Their ideas were not different from other ethnicities in the Republic of South Sudan, and my thanks go to them.

Finally, thanks go to my relatives and family for their sacrifices because joining the opposition side and voicing the truth put my life and their lives at risk. They never complain about being at risk because they understand that we have to make sacrifices in order to build our country. Special thanks to my wife and my kids, who helped find information and provided emotional support. As the sons and daughters of the WBG region, my family members were very concerned about the wrong direction in which the ruling elites were taking our country.

With so much support from the leaders and the people of the WBG, as well as my family, I can claim credit for being the first to document these historical events in a book.

INTRODUCTION

Globally, ethnic violence increasingly has become a serious threat to humankind and has caused the death of many. The acts of violence, which are sometimes considered triggers of insurgence, have been fuelled by ethnic tensions between groups that have different ethnic backgrounds. Identifying the causes of these ethnic tensions would likely result in finding a way to eliminate them, which would greatly contribute to a peaceful coexistent and go a long way to achieving a more peaceful world.

Governments around the world, faced with ethnic tension, would probably encounter insurgency. Therefore in the search for peaceful coexistence, leaders need to understand the historical propensities that will have to be considered before attempting to resolve the insurgency issues. Understanding the ethnic conflict in the heated countries, such as the Republic of South Sudan, would help other countries that are vulnerable to the same tensions avoid the conflict.

The conflict that started in South Sudan on 15 December 2013 has deep roots which could be traced back to the 1950s and the 1980s. The civil war, which had a combination of complex disagreements amongst the communities in the Republic of South Sudan, had historical causes. It is true that the drivers of this conflict for some ethnic groups were, for instance, a demand for legitimate rights and a struggle in order to survive in the motherland. Moreover, the causes of this conflict also were a demand for fairer representation for others. Unfortunately, the triggers of the civil war in the country were also caused by an attempt for dominance, power, access to resources, and ultimate control by a few people.

To many marginalised communities in the country, such as the Fertit community, grievances weren't born of the 2013 civil war but dated back to previous events, since the southern part of Sudan was created, linking historical issues to the post-2013 conflict.

The Fertit ethnic groups were caught in the above category. Similar to other communities across the Republic of South Sudan, the Fertit community has been opposing the regime in Juba since the independence of the country. The reason for their opposition dated back to before the independence of Sudan in the 1950s. Although some of the Fertit's aspirations were identical to the SPLM/A-IO's national agenda, other demands are attached to the earlier grievances that the Fertit community has suffered through for decades. Resolving that specific demand would grant the whole country needed stability.

It is true that since the independence of the Sudan on 1 January 1956, the reasons for the Fertit community to forcefully take up arms were specific to their perception of the history and developments of power dynamics across the southern part of Sudan, particularly across the WBG region.

Understanding the Fertit's perception of these historical events and how these events affected them is key to understanding the root causes of their opposition to the government, which in turn is crucial to any attempts to establish sustainable peace and coexistence amongst the inhabitants of South Sudan.

It is worth mentioning that the Fertit opposition to South Sudan's government is rooted in their demand for the right to live in safety, preserve their culture, and control their own resources. The Fertit opposition was born out of marginalisation and the facts that members of the ruling party, predominantly the Jieng community, are continuously attempting to seize control of the historical motherland of Fertit, the WBG region.

This has intensified by the reorganisation of South Sudan into controversial twenty-eight states in 2015 and thirty-two states in 2017, which has changed the demographic balance of Raja area in favour of the Jieng community by specifically annexing Raja to Aweil to become the controversial Lol state, making the indigenous Fertit a minority in their ancestral lands.

The Fertit Lion Forces joined the Sudan People's Liberation Movement/

Army-in-Opposition (SPLM/A-IO), under the leadership of Dr Riek Machar, in August 2014. By forming an alliance with the SPLM/A-IO, the Fertit aimed to unite with their follow citizens in calling for needed reform.

The 12 September 2018 Revitalised Agreement on the Resolution of the Conflict in the Republic of South Sudan R-ARCSS between the government and opposition parties was a good sign. However, the violations of the R-ARCSS by the government, specifically in the WBG region, continued to undermine the effectiveness of the resolution of the conflict.

The R-ARCSS is a golden chance for the Southern Sudanese leaders to redirect their country to a sustainable development, which was enjoyed shortly after the independence of the country. The likelihood that the R-ARCSS will deliver sustainable peace across the country is high. However, opposition and armed struggle against the government are likely to continue, in particular in the WBG region, if the local issues that fuelled armed resistance are not addressed in the future.

Overview

The War of Destiny is the first to document the challenges that were facing the Fertit community and how they survived the well-planned atrocities. Therefore the book is considered to be historical because the history of the region has not been documented. This book also is historical because it is an invitation to others to expand, supplement, and (if necessary) correct the information herein, in order to explore on the historical event and further background about the reason why the Fertit community became insurgent. This study will lead to identifying ways to prevent the ethnic tensions, and therefore conflicts, in the future, both in the country and around the world.

Traditional studies of ethnic violence focus on the details of historical animosities, economic disparities, leadership, or social structures of different regions. This book is unique in the way that it identifies the core causes of the ethnic conflict in the WBG region. *The War of Destiny* relies primarily on my personal notes and other leaders' notes, interviews with influential Fertit individuals, and secondary literature. Interviews with Fertit leaders took place during my several trips to the Sudan and the South Sudan since 2015.

Most of the interviewees were identified as Fertit leaders who have knowledge of WBG history, including traditional chiefs, Members of Parliament, military commanders, religious leaders, activists, and few previous government officials.

Interviewees were from various Fertit subethnic groups, mainly Balanda, Kresh, Banda, Feroghe, Ndogo, and Bongo, as well as also members of the Luo ethnic background. The interviewees were chosen to contribute because of their presence at the events mentioned in the book, specifically the establishment of the Fertit forces during the mid-eighties and 2000s in different number of villages in the Fertit area, surrounding Raja and Wau. Nearly all interviews were in local languages, Arabic, or English.

This research-based book has explored the background of the ethnic violence against the Fertit group and their reaction by forming organised forces in the WBG region. The book predicts civilians' propensity to more self-defence only if they were subjected to a large scale of grievances. This insight provides guidance for how the worst of ethnic violence can be prevented, even in other parts of the world with different cultures.

The results of this study are especially relevant today, and students, social science researchers, political and military leaders, and interested citizens at all levels should read the book. It documents the ethnic unrest that happened in the WBG region. *The War of Destiny* should also be recommended reading for officers and elites in the Republic of South Sudan and other parts of the world, where the possibility of ethnic conflicts amongst communities exist. The lesson learned from this book is applicable in the future, in order to prevent ethnic conflict and build a sustainable, peaceful coexistence around the world. There is a strong believe that *The War of Destiny* can bring about conflict prevention and could contribute to global peace building.

PART 1

The Militia Formation in the Western Bahr el Ghazal

The Second Sudanese Civil War was fought between the central Sudanese government and the resistance movement of the Sudan People's Liberation Movement and Army (SPLM/A) from 1983 to 2005. It was largely a continuation of the First Sudanese Civil War of Anya-Nya I, which began in 1955 and ended in 1972 with the Addis Ababa Agreement. During the second civil war, many counterinsurgent tribal militias emerged in the southern part of Sudan.

Claims by some individuals give the impression that formations of these tribal militias were planned under supervision of the government in Khartoum. The claim by Jieng aimed to give the perception that it was the policy of the government of Sudan to create a counterinsurgency against the SPLM/A. A counterinsurgency (COIN) can be defined as the process in which a group of civilians has been trained by a conventional army to defeat and contain insurgency and address its root causes. This is not true in the case of the Fertit militia.

The insurgency definition led observers to dig deep into the way the Fertit established their militia. Focusing on the establishment of the Fertit militia in 1985 and the given statements by Fertit tribal leaders, this book challenges the assumption that the Fertit militia was initially formed as a counterinsurgency. The book concludes that the emergence of the Fertit militia was principally a grassroots phenomenon as a result of violence against the Fertit by the SPLA, which was predominately comprised of the Jieng ethnic.

With tribal militia formations in the southern part of the Sudan, including that of the Fertit, the Sudanese government eventually used locally organised armed groups to assist in counterinsurgency during the civil war. But most important, the formation of Fertit militias emerged as a result of SPLA aggressions against the Fertit community, with decision-making at the local level carried out by the Fertit activists and tribal leaders. The Fertit decided to form their militia to defend themselves.

Fertit leaders mobilised their follow ethnicities for the militia after they had experienced SPLA violence and believed that the SPLA units were responsible for committing the aggressions against them. Fuelled by the SPLM/A violence and in fear of future attacks, local citizens of Fertit organised militia forces to defend and protect their innocent civilians and properties from SPLA forces.

These militia forces were organised around villages surrounding the provincial capital of Wau and in the south-west of Raja County. After the formation of the militias, they were used to protect Fertit civilians and their properties. But the Fertit militias have also been used to engage in counterattacks against Jieng ethnic rivals who were deemed to be responsible for the initial cycles of violence that instigated instability in the whole Western Bahr el Ghazal (WBG) region.

Western Bahr el Ghazal

Historically, the WBG region has been home to Fertit ethnic groups going back to before the 1600s. The region has been named Dar Fertit as well as Dar Fur in the Republic of Sudan. The slave trades were largely a threat and common in the Dar Fertit or WBG region. The region experienced the first raids for slave in the 1700s by Muslim sultanates. Interestingly, although Dar Fertit went through slavery, many different ethnicities from Northern Sudan and Western Sudan, especially Dar Fur, took refuge in the Dar Fertit region, where they escaped from violence and slavery.

When the Republic of Sudan gained its independence in 1956, the Sudan inherited nine regions from the Angelo-Egyptian administration in 1948. The Sudanese regions stood on the Angelo-Egyptian borders and encompassed Bahr el Ghazal, Blue Nile, Darfur, Equatoria, Kassala, Khartoum, Kordofan, Northern, and Upper Nile. These nine Sudanese regions remained until 1975. The number of the region was increased to become eighteen in 1976. By 1991, the Sudan began to adopt a federal structure of nine states corresponding to the nine former historic regions, with the Bahr el Ghazal becoming its own region. The Bahr el Ghazal encompassed Buhairat, North Bahr el Ghazal, and Western Bahr el Ghazal. Further division happened on 14 February 1994, when the Sudan government increased the number of states to twenty-six, with the southern part of Sudan composed of ten states and the Western Bahr el Ghazal separated to become its own state. The ten southern states became part of independent South Sudan on 9 July 2011.

The Fertit ethnic group has being living together under one administration, with Jieng and Luo ethnicities in the Bahr el Ghazal region, since the British colonial era. The first ethnic tensions amongst Fertit and Jieng started during the Torit Mutiny in 1955 and reoccurred after the Addis Ababa Agreement in 1972. As a result of these ethnic tensions, in 1974, under the government of Sudan and President Jaafar Muhammad Al Nimiery, a technical committee was formed to provide recommendations on restructuring the southern districts in order to reduce the ethnic tensions and accelerate the development of social and economic sectors in the southern part of Sudan. The aim of re-establishing the southern part of Sudan was also for the establishment of local administrations in order to help with the management of the regions. Based on the consultation by the technical committee, in 1983 the southern part of Sudan was restructured into three regions: Upper Nile, Equatoria, and Bahr el Ghazal.

Although Bahr el Ghazal was established, in its recommendation, the technical committee raised its concerns about the gathering of different ethnic groups, such as the Jieng, Fertit, and Luo, with different cultures in one region.

Since its creation, different cultures were experienced in the Bahr el Ghazal. For instance, conflict began between Jieng pastoralists and Fertit and Luo farmers over grazing. Also, Jiengs dominated the local government posts, preventing the needed development in the area inhabited mostly by Fertit ethnic groups. One example of this culture differences problem was Jieng officials mismanaging the agriculture bank loan offered by the government of President Jaafar Muhammad Al Nimiery to the farmers who appeared to be Fertits.

As a result, on 10 December 1982, the Western Bahr el Ghazal Development Committee was created. It petitioned the president of Sudan, Jaafar Muhammad Al Nimiery, in a letter recommending the establishment of the Western Bahr el Ghazal (WBG) region. The committee included Darius Bashir, Hillary Akuang, Ali Tamim Fartak, Donato Mabior, Musa Dayia, Stephan Akot, Jacinto Lee Zeki, Ceaser Zemangi, and Joseph Akul. The committee demanded the WBG region be separated because the Jieng committed corruption, domination, and marginalisation against the Fertit ethnic groups.

The WBG region was then created on the Angelo-Egyptian borders. The region has borders with South Darfur to the north-west, the Central African Republic to the south-west, Aweil in the north-east, Gogrial and Tonj in the east, and the Yampio to the south. The WBG territory, which was considered the motherland of the Fertit community, is largely fertile and flat and includes many water resources.

The Western Bahr el Ghazal region, per the boundaries of 1 January 1956, consisted of three major areas: Wau, Jur River, and Raja (including Kafia Kingi). The WBG region has an area estimated as 93,900 square kilometres, with Raja considered the largest area in the region with 61,793 square kilometres. Wau has 19,951 square kilometres, and Jur River has 10,732 square kilometres.

The region is rich in the following natural resources.

- Agriculture, such as sorghum, sesame, beans, coffee, maize, cassava, soya, groundnut, mango, guava, lemon, banana, tomato, okra, eggplant, pumpkin, tobacco, sweet potato, and beehive
- Forestry, such as mahogany and other kinds of woods
- Mineral, such as iron and copper

Natives of the region are mainly the Luo tribe and the Fertit ethnic group, and these include twenty-seven ethnicities that can be classified as Bantus. The region is also inhabited by the Jieng of Marial Baii.

The Fertit Group

Earlier in the history of Sudan, Fertit was a name for a group of ethnic tribes that represented non-Jieng, non-Arab, non-Luo, and non-Fur groups. Before the British colonised the Republic of Sudan, in the 1820s the Turco-Egyptians established military control over the northern part of Sudan as they sought to achieve their dreams of gaining natural resources, trades, and economic expansion.

However, the Turco-Egyptian administration did not attempt to enter the southern part of the Sudan, and this part remained isolated for many years. In 1841, the Turco-Egyptian administration, accompanied by Arabs from the north, decided to enter the territory of the south for exploitation of the animal and human resources, represented by ivory and slaves, respectively. The southern part of Sudan included the Upper Nile, where there were swamplands known as the Sudd, and the areas farther south and east in the Western Bahr el Ghazal region, where there were forests and mountains.

The Turco-Egyptian administration then allowed northern traders to enter the southern part, particularly Fertit land. Al Zubeir Rahma Mansur arrived in the Western Bahr el Ghazal. Although the Fertit land was seasonally experiencing slavery, during the Turco-Egyptian administration, the Fertit suffered most from the slave trade by Al Zubeir Rahma Mansur and its army in 1865.

Al Zubeir was a Sudanese trader who initially went to the WBG region for ivory and gum arabic. However, Al Zubeir turned to brutally, catching South Sudanese (and especially Fertit) civilians and trading them as slaves when his attempt to trade in the region became unsuccessful. During his brutal slave trade, Al Zubeir gathered slaves around the town of Uyujuku; its name was later changed to Deim Zubeir. Deim Zubeir became an important centre and the clearing house of the slave industry. It is worth mentioning that slave raiding had been practised in the area before Al Zubeir violently intensified it.

Moreover, the presence of the Turco-Egyptian administration in the Republic of Sudan created conditions favourable to the growth of a radically Muslim ideology, led by Muhammad Ahmed Ibn Abdullah, who gained his popularity in 1881 and declared himself Muhammad Ahmad Al Mahdi.

Al Mahdi was considered a founding father of Sudan because he had fundamental role in the early Sudanese fighting for independence. He commanded an army in order to fight the invaders, and by 1885 Al Mahdi had liberated most of the Sudanese territory. In that year, his forces captured Khartoum, and Al Mahdi established a theocratic Mahdist state. The theocratic Mahdist government lasted until the Anglo-Egyptian forces invaded the Sudan. Unfortunately, the slave trade continued to increase in the WGB region under the radical Islamic Mahdist rule.

The Fertit encompassed about twenty-seven ethnicities, and the larger ones were Balanda, Banda, Kresh, Ndogo, Golo, Bai, Feroghe Bongo, and Cere. Other ethnicities who were also considered to be Fertit were Falata and Azande. These tribes have diverse geographical origins, with some coming from Darfur and others from the Central African Republic. The Fertit speak various languages, but most can communicate in Arabic or English. The Fertit have mostly engaged in traditional agriculture, fishing, and hunting. The major religions of the Fertit ethnic groups are Christianity and Islam, with Roman Catholicism representing the most, and a few Protestants.

The Fertit live in the WBG region and parts of Western Equatoria. Prior to the Anglo-Egyptian administration in the Sudan, particularly during the Al Mahdi caliphs, the history of the Fertit was marked by oppression, slave raiding, and uncertain rule.

As a result of the growing economic, political, and social corruption in the reign of Al Mahdi caliphs under the succession of Muhammad Ahmad Al Mahdi, in 1898, Anglo-Egyptian combined forces were able to defeat Al Mahdi forces, gain control of Sudan after the Omdurman battle, and colonise the country. The invading troops, under the Command of Herbert Kitchener, took control of the capital city of Khartoum.

The Anglo-Egyptian then expanded its forces and took full control of Sudan territories in 1899. By then, the Fertit still were subjected to looting and slave raiding, mostly from Arab tribes from the north. Unfortunately, the new administration of the Anglo-Egyptian introduced no specific antislavery measures in the WBG region during the early stages of the condominium period.

In fact, the Anglo-Egyptian administration originally had no physical presence in the WBG region, especially in the north-west of the region. That led to a lack of any kind of government administration and security, which resulted in uncertainty in the region.

During the second half of the condominium period, British district officers began to protect the Fertit ethnic groups and strengthening British administration in the WBG region by relocating Fertit ethnic groups to be near the roads. They drew a border between the northern and southern parts of the Sudan.

The colonial administration then began to introduce specific measures in the southern part. In light of the southern policy by British administration, the Arabic language and Islam were discouraged, and Catholic missionaries were invited to increase their presence in the area. As this was implemented in the whole southern part of Sudan, many northern Arabs were prevented from entering the WBG region, or they were expelled. Additionally, Fertit chiefs and their followers were advised by British administration to abandon their Arabic names and their Arabic style of dress.

CHAPTER 2

Fertit Role in the First Sudanese Civil War

During the Anglo-Egyptian administration era, in the 1940s the Anglo-Egyptian administration decided to maintain a border of the Southern part of the Sudan. Therefore in 1946, the Anglo-Egyptian administration, under a condominium governing arrangement, administered the Southern part and the Northern part of the Sudan as separate regions. The two areas were then merged into a single administrative region as part of British strategy.

This arrangement was implemented without consultation with southern leaders, who feared being absorbed by the political power of the larger, educated population in north. The southern part of Sudan was inhabited primarily by Christians and traditional African believers, and it considered itself culturally African, whereas most of the inhabitants in the northern part of the Sudan were Muslims who were culturally Islam and Arab.

In the earlier stage, prior to independence, the Southerners accused British officials of not attempting to safeguard the interests of Southerners or prevent the Northerners from gaining dominance over them. As the country prepared for independence, in June 1953 the Cairo Conference was organised in order to discuss the future of the country. Unfortunately, the Southerners had been marginalised from this process by the leaders in the North.

In addition, the Northern elites began to view the Southerners as second-class citizens, and the Northerners differentiated themselves as the sons of the Sudan. The Southerners were not considered by Northern elites as the real sons of the country, and therefore Southern opinions were not taking seriously or even consulted in any decision-making process. In fact, before independence in the 1950s, when there were massive discussions on the future of the country, Southerners were not continuously included.

Furthermore, during the Sudanization Program, the Sudanese Committee, which was responsible for the appointment of civil servants in Sudan, allocated most key positions in the Southern part to Northern officials. In February 1954, Southerners felt openly cheated when only six junior administrative posts in the Southern part were allocated to them, whereas eight hundred public posts went to Northerners. Meanwhile, their consistent demand for federal status was not taken seriously by the Northerners.

As a result of Southerners being excluded from the political and economic activities in the country, eventually the Southerner uprising began with the Torit Mutiny on 18 August 1955. The Torit Mutiny was considered the first rebellion of the Southerners against Arabs in the North. Pastor Saturnino Lohure commanded the mutineers to demand equal representation for the Southerners. The mutiny paved the way later to the foundation of Anya-Nya I movement.

It was the first time that Southerners openly protested against the policy and treatment by both the Anglo-Egyptian administration and the Arab North against them. The Southerners protested what they consider Anglo-Egyptian policy that favoured Northern Sudanese Arabs. The Fertit supported the mutineers in the early stage, joined the Anya-Nya I in large numbers, and were involved in waging successful guerrilla attacks against the Northern troops throughout the Bahr el Ghazal.

In February 1953, when the Anglo-Egyptian administration made an agreement to grant independence to Sudan, the internal tensions over the future nature of the relationship between the Northerners and Southerners were heightened. The Northerners were asked to grant the Southern part of the Sudan a federal system of governance. Unfortunately, when independence day, 1 January 1956, approached, the Northern leaders backed away from commitments to create a federal government system that would give the Southern part of the country substantial autonomy.

This lack of commitment from the Northerners resulted in the disagreement between North and South. The disagreement became the first Sudanese Civil War, which was between the first Sudanese administration in the North and the Anya-Nya I rebellion, which represented the Southern part of the Sudan.

The Sudanese Civil War started with the Torit Mutiny in 1955 and ended with the Addis Ababa Agreement in 1972. The Anya-Nya I demanded fair representation and more regional autonomy in the Southern part of the country. Anya-Nya is a phrase from one of Southern Sudanese tribes, Madi, which means *snake venom*.

The Fertit ethnic groups, who joined the Torit mutineers with the large numbers, were quick to participate in Anya-Nya I movement and become active soldiers. The Fertit leaders were represented in the high command of the movement.

However, the government of Sudan, under the leadership of President Jaafar Muhammad Al Nimiery, dishonoured the Addis Ababa Agreement. As a result, the agreement that ended the first Sudanese civil war in 1972 failed to grant the Southern part of the Sudan federalism, and it failed to completely address the root causes of the conflict and eliminate the tensions that had originally caused it, leading to a reigniting of the North-South conflict during the Second Sudanese Civil War, which started in 1983 and ended in 2005 with the Comprehensive Peace Agreement (CPA) between the government in the North and the SPLM/A.

Clement Mboro

At the beginning, there were several Southern Sudanese officials who demanded rights for their people during the first civil war. One of them was Clement Mboro, who was one of the few Western Bahr el Ghazal WBG intellectuals during the Anya-Nya I movement.

As an intellectual, Clement Mboro was the only person from the WBG region present during the Juba Conference of 1947, and he was amongst the only three educated Southerners to participate in the conference.

At a time when many Southerners were given low-skilled jobs, Clement Mboro held several administrative posts. He was appointed assistant district commissioner of Yirol. Unfortunately, he was detained and tortured following the Torit Mutiny in 1955 due to his support for the mutineers, who refused to be transported to North Sudan and revolted against their Northern commanding officers. The move led to a large-scale conflict and saw many Southern civilians, soldiers, and politicians (including Mr Mboro) face persecution and even death.

After his arrest, Clement Mboro was tried in the court on fabricated charges and sentenced to eighteen months' imprisonment. Mboro's time in prison was then extended to ten years, and he was flown to Khobar Prison in North Sudan. He was released after serving two years.

Upon his release from prison, Mboro regained employment and became the district commissioner of Juba in 1957. Three years later in 1960, he was imprisoned again in Juba for two years and released in 1962. Clement held several positions: secretary of the Darfur Province, deputy commissioner of Port Sudan, and deputy governor of Darfur in 1964.

As a politician and an activist who was advocating for the interests of his people, Clement Mboro and other Southerners formed a political movement known as the Southern Front. He became president of the party and had a substantial role in developing and providing facilities and financial assistance to the party, ensuring the opinions of Southerners were heard.

Clement Mboro was a vocal voice of South Sudanese, and he became popular amongst his people. When he visited Southern Sudan in 1964, people travelled from various regions of the South just to hear his message. Many people gathered at the airport on 6 December 1964, the day he was scheduled to return to Khartoum after the end of his tour in the South.

With the constant turn of political events, and following the military coup in Sudan in 1969, General Jaafar Muhammad Al Nimiery became president of the Sudan. Because of his political activities, the Al Nimiery regime sentenced Clement Mboro to life imprisonment, and Mboro was sent once again to Khobar Prison in May 1969. However, he was released in 1972 during the Addis Ababa Agreement, and he regained his position as a leading voice amongst Southern politicians. On 7 July 2006, Mr Clement passed away in Nairobi, Kenya.

Ferdinand Goi Ukelo

Pastor Ferdinand Goi Ukelo was one of the most fearless Anya-Nya I military commanders who emerged from the WBG region at that time of the First Sudanese Civil War. Immediately after the independence of the Sudan, the Anya-Nya I became emerged stronger and became an umbrella of several Southern opposition movements, including the Sudan African National Union (SANU) party. Ferdinand Goi was a commander-in-chief and the chairman of the Sudan African National Union party.

In his efforts to unite the people in the southern part of the Sudan behind the movement, on 9 November 1964, Major Ferdinand wrote a letter to the Southern Sudanese people asking them to depend on themselves in their struggle to liberate their country. He asked the citizens who possessed guns to offer their guns to the Any-Nya I soldiers. His active role in mobilising support of the movement resulted in the Anya-Nya I receiving resources from the Southern Sudanese people. These efforts allowed the Anya- Nya I to sustain the war against the North.

Ukelo also had a role in mobilising internationally. Before he died, he visited Italy in March 1970. His visit to Italy lasted for three months, and he met with reporters and Italian people who were considered friends of Southern Sudanese, in order to mobilise political and financial support for the movement. During his visit to Italy, as a result of his meeting with many Italian friends, the Anya-Nya I was able to gain resources such as money, clothes, military uniforms, and medical supplies, which were successfully transferred back to help the movement, under the command of Colonel Joseph Lagu.

General Joseph Yakobo Lagu, a member of the Madi tribe, was the chairman of the Southern Sudan Liberation Movement (SSLM) and the commander-in-chief of the Anya-Nya armed forces. Joseph Lagu played a major role in the rise and consolidation of the Anya-Nya movement.

Picture of Ferdinand Goi (1970)

Unfortunately, Ferdinand Goi suffered from a heart condition, malaria, and sleeping sickness. As a result, Major Ferdinand died in St Mary's Hospital of Gulu, Uganda, on 9 November 1970.

He was first amongst the Southern to call for a free and independent Southern Sudan. An Italian reporter, Giorgio Rapanelli, who accompanied Major Ferdinand Goi, described Ferdinand as a fearless commander, attacking conveys of the Northern Sudanese army in their stronghold. As such, the government in the North placed a high bounty on his life.

Ukelo cooperated with an Italian photographer in order to document and report on various activities of the Anya-Nya I. This let the world know about the first war for independence of the South Sudan.

Despite his tremendous contribution to his country, Ukelo never asked privileges for himself. He asked his friends only for batteries for the tape recorder he was using to listen to his favourite classical music, especially Johann Sebastian Bach.

Early Tension in Greater Bahr el Ghazal

After the independence of the Sudan, the Bahr el Ghazal region was already inhabited by several main ethnic groups, including the Jiengs, the Fertit, and the Luo. The Jiengs were mainly pastoralists who performed very little cultivation. The Jieng tribe, which was the largest tribe of the Bahr el Ghazal region, occupied the former Aweil District, north-west of Wau town; the Gogrial District, north of Wau; part of the Jur River District; Tonj, which is north-east of Wau; and the Lakes District in the east.

The Fertit group and the Luo ethnic group occupied the Western District, with the Fertit ethnic groups dominant in the south and west of Wau town and up to Raja in the far west, the area bordering Central Africa Republic (CAR) and the Darfur region to the North.

The Luo inhabited the land in the borders of Wau District between the Jieng tribe and Fertit ethnic groups, which was east, north, and north-west of Wau. Although the Fertit and Luo ethnicity were mainly farmers, they also kept a few cattle and goats.

Wau had been the provincial headquarters of Bahr el Ghazal since the colonial era, and it eventually became the regional capital of Western Bahr el Ghazal State (WBGS) in February 1994. It then became its own separated state on 2 October 2015.

Tensions between the Jieng and Fertit ethnic groups started before the independence of Sudan. The first ethnic tension emerged at the time of the Torit Mutiny, which took place on 18 August 1955. During the time of the Torit Mutiny, members of the Fertit ethnic group were the first to join the mutineers and later the Anya-Nya I forces, and they became the only insurgents in the area of the Bahr el Ghazal. Some members of the Fertit community, who joined the struggle against the central government in North, were responsible for the attacks on army convoys in the area of Bahr el Ghazal, including the areas the Jiengs inhabited. As a result of the Fertit soldiers attacking the Northern army around Jieng lands, the Jieng had a strong disliking for the Fertit.

In the earlier stages of the First Sudanese Civil War, most of the Jieng remained contemptuously distanced from the Anya-Nya I movement. Also, members of Jieng ethnicity greatly facilitated repression against the Anya-Nya I soldiers in the Bahr el Ghazal area.

Moreover, after the Addis Ababa agreement, which took place on 27 February 1972, the situation in Bahr el Ghazal featured tribalism, nepotism, marginalisation, and discrimination against the Fertit.

Huge numbers of the Fertit ethnic groups were fully active soldiers of the Anya-Nya I, and they had been fighting for equal representation and federalism. After the Addis Ababa agreement, unfortunately they were sidelined, disarmed, and demobilised during the process of absorption. Most Fertit soldiers who were Anya-Nya guerrillas were laid off, and the Jieng were absorbed into the national army instead. This act contributed to the already deteriorating ethnic tension between the two groups.

Further reason for the worsening of the ethnic tension between the Jieng and Fertit community was that after the signing of the Addis Ababa Agreement, the Arabs in North allocated higher positions in the South to members of the Jieng. As a result, Fertit leaders became frustrated about the fact that although the Jieng did not participate in the uprising against the North, the Jieng received a disproportionate number of government jobs. Members of Jieng ethnicity indeed occupied higher administrative positions, which should have gone to the numerically smaller group of educated Fertit as a reward for their participation in the fight for equal rights for the Southerners.

To give some few examples, in the first local government of the Bahr el Ghazal region, out of seven minsters, six were members of the Jieng ethnic tribe, one was from Luo, and the Fertit were excluded from local government. Furthermore, junior Jieng officials were given promotions over the Fertit senior officials. The marginalisation of Fertit led them to accuse the Jieng of tribalism, nepotism, and malpractice.

Apart from the above mentioned Jieng policy of marginalisation and domination, another immediate cause for the worsening of ethnic tension between Jiang and Fertit involved the allocation of public resources. When the new administration was established in the capital of the Bahr el Ghazal. Wau, after the Addis Ababa Agreement, a Ministerial Committee was appointed by the governor in order to distribute government houses to senior officials of the regional government. The committee was made of two Jieng ministers with a Luo minister as the chairman. The committee became biased in their distribution and allotment of public resources, such as government houses, vehicles, and lands. These public resources were mostly allocated to the Jieng officials.

Another ethnic tension was the way the regional government distributed plots in and around Wau, which was Fertit land. The lands were allocated only to Jieng officials. Further, other land, such as the new plots in market area, was demarcated, surveyed, and distributed only to Jieng traders and a few Northern traders.

When the state government decided to demarcate, survey, and distribute the land falling on the Jur River's banks to senior government officials for cultivation and countryside homes, they were also allocated mostly to Jieng officials.

As a result of unfair distribution of jobs and public resources immediately after the Addis Ababa Agreement, ethnic tensions increased, following by Fertit demands for creation of a separate WBG region from the Bahr el Ghazal region, with the formation of a new regional government that excluded the Jieng community.

Citing a report from the Committee for the Redivision of the Southern Provinces, The Fertit had an intense feeling against the Jieng, and there was strong aspiration for a separate province. The Fertit were afraid of being continuously marginalised and dominated by the Jieng. Similar tensions and demands occurred in Equatoria in the 1970s and early 1980s.

As a result, in the first stage of the Second Civil War, started in 1983, only a few Fertit joined the new rebellion led by the SPLA, although more Fertit joined it later. Many Southerners, including a large number of

Fertit, first perceived the SPLM/A as a Jieng movement and believed that the Jieng used the SPLM/A as a vehicle for establishing Jieng hegemony in Southern Sudan. This belief was, in part, the result of the fact that many of the earlier SPLM/A recruiters and high officers were Jieng. Also, some Fertit leaders chose to not join the SPLM/A because of the purportedly unfair distribution of jobs after the first civil war. As a result, the majority of Fertit ethnic groups hesitated to join the SPLM/A, and therefore the SPLA commanders considered them a hostile group.

CHAPTER 4

SPLA Aggressions Against Fertit Civilians in WBG

Raja County

Aside from the aftermath ethnic tension that the Torit Mutiny caused, tensions between the Fertit and the Jieng in Bahr el Ghazal occurred after both the independence of Sudan in 1956 and the Addis Ababa Agreement in 1972. The Fertit were being discriminated again by Jiengs, who increasingly dominated the administration posts in both the Bahr el Ghazal region and Southern Sudan. These tensions worsened after the SPLM/A, a predominantly Jieng ethnic tribe, started an uprising against the Sudanese government in 1983.

The SPLM/A, under the leadership of its chairman and commander-in-chief, Dr John Garang de Mabior, engaged mostly in guerrilla warfare all over the Sudan, particularly in the southern, eastern, and western parts of the country. During the twenty-one years of civil war, the movement attacked police stations, army outposts, and military convoys around the country. However, the military wing of the SPLM/A, the SPLA, had its main presence in the Southern part of Sudan. In these places, the SPLA units relied on civilians for the supply of food, clothes, human resources, and other materials.

Therefore in some cases, the SPLA commanders approached village leaders peacefully, asking them mostly for food supplies. In other situation, as in the areas around Wau and Raja, sometimes writing as Raga, the SPLA commanders or unit members used forces to gain access to food supplies and other materials.

At the first stage of the establishment of the SPLM/A, the period between 1983 and 1987, there were high rates of violence against Fertit ethnic groups by the SPLA soldiers. The SPLA soldiers committed violence against unarmed Fertit civilians around Wau and Raja city. The SPLA soldiers perceived members of Fertit groups hostile to the SPLM/A, which appears to have been the reason why Fertits were specifically vulnerable to SPLA aggressions.

In 1985 and 1986, the SPLA focused most of its attacks on civilian populations deemed hostile in Jonglei, Equatoria, and the Bahr el Ghazal region. Therefore although other tribes experienced attacks by the SPLA units, the Murle, Toposa, Mundari, and Fartit ethnic groups especially suffered most amongst the Southern ethnic groups.

In 1985, the SPLA were relocated specifically to the Fertit villages in the south-west of Wau and the south of Raja County. Then the Fertit ethnic groups were targeted and became subjected to the SPLA's violent raids. Looting, violence, and rape were the most common forms of aggression during the raids by SPLA soldiers. The raids occurred during the rainy season at the time of cultivation, causing fear amongst the Fertit famers in the villages around Wau and Raja. Civilians were terrorised by SPLA violence.

Villagers also suffered from sexual violence, forceful abduction, and killings. During that period, there were many unarmed Fertit civilians who were killed by SPLA soldiers. Usually it was a part of searching for food supplies; when they raided these villages, the SPLA would take women to rape, as well as underage girls.

In order to clear their way and feel safe, the SPLA attacked all government military spots around Wau and Raja. Specifically, on 24 July 1986 they violently attacked Deim Zubeir and burnt the police station. They shot and murdered twenty people, burnt seven commercial lorries, looted properties, and abducted thirty people, including two tribal chiefs (Chief William Didi and Chief Michael Mahmoud).

The local tribal leaders have confirmed the identities of the attackers as SPLA soldiers, and the soldiers generally had physical characteristics of the Jieng ethnicity. From their language and the way the SPLA soldiers communicated, tribal leaders believed that the assailants were Jieng, specifically from the area of Aweil.

In the earlier stages of the SPLM/A establishment, in the 1980s, youth from the area of Aweil were quick to join the SPLM/A in large numbers. For many Jieng from Aweil, the main reason to join the movement was to gain arms and military training in order to protect their lands from the Rizeiqat and Misseriya.

Also, the members of the Jieng community were taking advantage of being soldiers in order to seek revenge against whomever they considered to be their opponents. In the case of Raja and Wau, some Fertit leaders believed that SPLA soldiers, specifically from Aweil, were using the civil war context to take revenge against Fertit. Others believed that these soldiers were taking advantage of being SPLA to commit crimes. As a result, some Fertit civilians described their attackers as robbers who were part of the SPLA, accusing them of not really carrying out the mission and vision of the SPLM/A, which was under the leadership of Dr John Garang de Mabior. Assailants may have been officially considered members of the insurgency, but they were not genuinely committed to the moral principles of the SPLM/A.

Wau County

Similarly, at the time of the first raids on the villages around Raja County by the SPLA, there were also systematic attacks on unarmed Fertit civilians in the urban area and villages surrounding Wau. The attacks were characterised by Fertit leaders as a form of collective punishment for the Fertit ethnic group's failure to join the SPLA, The reason for past tension between Fertit and Jieng at the time of the First Sudanese Civil War, when the Fertit were the first to join the Torit mutineers, automatically becoming Anya-Nya I soldiers in the Bahr el Ghazal.

Some Fertit tribal leaders noted that violence was due to the fact that Fertit ethnic groups had, after the Addis Ababa Agreement, protested against the dominance of the Jieng in the WBG. The Jieng occupied higher administration positions. These SPLA soldiers, who were predominantly Jieng from Aweil, were upset, and they returned to reorganise themselves within the SPLA in order to take revenge and maintain their domination in the region.

Second, Fertit sources stated that the raids were part of a larger future plan for Jieng dominance. This view came up in the Jieng's conference in early 1985, in which they laid out their plan to politically and economically control Fertit land. During that meeting, the Jieng introduced two options as their plan to dominate the Fertit in the near future. The first option was for the Jieng to enter into massive intermarriage with Fertit women. The second option was for the Jieng to violently invade the Fertit land. Violently invading WGB land would be chosen if there was resistance to the first option.

As expected, because of the bitterness between the two communities, the plan of massive intermarriage between Jieng men and Fertit women failed, and the invasion of the Fertit land was chosen. Members of the neighbouring Luo tribe, particularly Jur Shatt, were also sometimes forced to be part of the violence against the Fertit villagers. In fact, because the Jieng did not know the WBG region, some elements of the Luo tribe, specifically the subtribe Jur Shatt, led the SPLA soldiers (predominantly Jieng) to the areas of the Fertit. Elements of Jur Shatt directed the SPLA units to Fertit houses and farms, where they looted, raped, and committed violence against unarmed civilians.

The SPLA aggression against Fertit ethnic groups was severe. The Fertit civilians were subjected to all kind of physical, sexual, psychological, and emotional abuses by the SPLA soldiers.

The SPLA soldiers committed violence against Fertit civilians in cold blood. In some cases, SPLA elements forced Fertit women to lie with their backs on top of their husbands, and then they raped them. Some Fertit women were physically abused after they had been raped.

As a result of the attacks, the Fertit began to hide their agricultural products. One case involved a SPLA soldier grabbing a Fertit child by her foot and hitting her head on a tree in order to force her parents to show them where they were hiding the crops. In another case, a soldier smashed a child in the traditional machine for producing peanut butter, called a fonduck.

Some Fertit were killed, and others suffered wholesale looting. Fertit leaders wondered how the SPLM/A claimed to be a liberated movement and yet was involved in the humiliation of their fellow citizens. How did they decide to attack the civilians whom they should have liberated? It gave Fertit leaders no doubt that they were being targeted by their opponent, the Jieng, for events in the past.

As a young boy, I personally witnessed my close relatives, Fertit civilians, fleeing from the Fertit villages to the town of Wau. Those who had been running from SPLA attacks included my uncles and their families. One of my uncles, Naei, and his wife sought refuge in my family's house. Naei explained how his wife was raped in front of him. One SPLA officer asked him if that was all right while another soldier raped his wife. Then, the solider forcefully raped Naei as will.

In 1986 there were systemic attacks on Fertit civilians in the villages around Raja and Wau by the SPLA forces, who were mainly Jieng. The SPLA units moved into the Fertit villages, looting their properties, raping women and men alike, killing some people, and committing atrocities in cold blood.

Below are a few examples of such incidents in the Fertit areas by the Jieng SPLA and the Nyigat, which is a predominantly Jieng police unit around that time, stationed in the Mapel area.

On 17 March 1986 at Taban village, around Kpaile area, the predominantly Jieng forces attacked the civilians, killed five persons, looted properties, and burnt fifteen houses.

On 29 April 1986 at both Getan and Ayo areas, the SPLA attacked innocent civilians, killed seven persons, looted properties, and burnt houses.

On 12 June 1986 at Momoi and Ngo Ngba, specifically on the Wau-Bussere road, the SPLA soldiers attacked and killed twenty-five civilians, looted properties, and burnt several houses.

On 15 June 1986 in the Kpaile area, they attacked the police station, killed twenty-three people, looted civilian properties, burnt civilian houses and shops, and abducted thirty men, women, and schoolgirls. As in other parts of Fertit villages, the abductees were forced to carry looted resources; afterwards, they were often raped, and sometimes they were freed.

On 27 June 1986 at Mboro, SPLA soldiers killed thirty-five innocent civilians in cold blood, looted properties, and burnt down several houses.

However, the SPLA officer who was in charge of this attack later wrote a letter to Chief Kamilo Gaki Mboro, apologizing to the surrounding communities and claiming that they had been misinformed there were Fertit militia in the area.

On 28 June 1986 at Ngo Mbolo and Rehan Fei, the SPLA killed fifteen civilians, looted properties, and burnt houses.

On 14 August 1986, SPLA soldiers attacked Wau and the surrounding area, which was densely populated by the Fertit community. The SPLA terrorised civilians, killed eleven people, looted properties, and burnt houses.

SPLA attacks continued in the Fertit villages of Bringi, Ugali, Ngo Ku, and Ngo Lengbo, as well as the Halima Research Station and the Abushaka area.

Immediately after the above-mentioned attacks by SPLA soldiers, the Fertit leaders contacted the SPLA military commander in charge in order to stop the violence. The SPLA commander denied waging war on the Fertit and instead accused the Nyigat police in the Mapel area of robbing, looting, and killing in the name of the SPLA. Nyigat were special police forces predominantly from the Jieng tribe.

The Fertit elders then petitioned the governor, Dr Lawrence Wol Wol, to provide protection for their people. The governor refused their demand and instead told them that the state government could not provide security for people in their houses and that it was up to the Fertit to provide their own security.

After the failure of the Fertit leaders to find a peaceful solution, the Fertit community decided to protect themselves. Initially, as it was in Raja, the Fertit youth in and around Wau picked up white weapons and arms to defend their innocent civilians and properties from attacks. They organised themselves into militia forces with white arms and tried to provide some kind of protection to their villages against both the Nyigat and the SPLA. Hence, it can be seen from this information that it was the SPLA soldiers, predominantly members of the Jieng tribe, who attacked Fertit. Later, the governor who denied the Fertit community the necessary government protection forced the Fertit to take up arms and protect themselves.

The Fertit developed their militia forces, chased the SPLA from their villages, and prevented further atrocities against them.

CHAPTER 5

Formation of Fertit Militia in the WBG Region

Around Raja County

Fertit leaders were under pressure as SPLA aggression continued, and they looked for a way to prevent the violence perpetrated against them. Following the SPLA raids, Fertit leaders in villages south of Raja, mostly from the Banda, Balanda, and Kresh, had a meeting in Deim Zubeir to discuss how to protect their women and children from SPLA attacks. The Fertit chiefs, the elders, and some activists discussed several options to protect themselves and their properties. Finally, the participants agreed on the idea of forming a militia as the best way to protect their villages.

At the early stage of militia mobilisation, meetings were done secretly in places such as homes and schools. Active civilians increasingly came to attend the meetings. Men, youths, and women came together to discuss the SPLA attacks and exchange ideas about how they could organise militia forces. The meetings lasted for a week, and a further agenda was discussed regarding how to obtain resources and basic military training for the volunteers.

On the final day of the meeting, the Fertit leaders decided to form the militia, and they collectively named their militia forces Qwat Salam, which mean "Peace Forces" in Arabic. The Fertit leaders then moved to implement what they agreed upon in the meeting. They also agreed on the most effective way to recruit, which was for the chiefs to ask every subtribe leader to help mobilise young tribesmen. As the Fertit people heard about the new militia recruitment in their neighbourhood, young men voluntarily joined the new forces in large numbers.

For those who lived in villages for decades, some Fertit civilians owned guns for hunting. In the early stages of the militia formation, those who owned guns joined with their guns. Others who did not possess guns primarily used spears, arrows, and machetes to protect their villages against SPLA attacks. For elderly Fertit members who could not join the militia but owned guns, they brought their guns to be used by others.

The collection of firearms took place at the village level, and the Fertit immediately used these guns. Also, when somebody in the village had one gun, then people with white arms regrouped with the owner of this gun. In general, if one family owned guns, then one of its members joined with their guns or gave them to the young people of the militia. Additionally, in order to increase the number of their guns, villagers began to purchase firearms.

After a few days, firearms were collected and made available. Eventually, the Fertit reorganised themselves and defended their villages. The militia forces started to capture weapons and ammunition from the SPLA units during their confrontations.

Accusation against Jur Shatt

The formation of the Fertit militia in the south of Raja County was asymmetrical. In the first stage of the Fertit organising militia, Sopo and Deim Zubeir were the first to form their militia forces, followed by Yabulu, Korhaga, and Korgana on the road from Deim Zubeir to Wau. All of the aforementioned villages that experienced SPLA raids in 1985 and 1986 created militia forces at the village level.

However, there were mistrust and internal issues amongst these villages, which led to the militia forces being formed at different times in these areas. In this regard, some inhabitants of Yabulu, Korgana, and Korhaga were from a Luo subtribe, Jur Shatt, which was known by the Thuri as well. They had been living together in these Fertit villages for decades, working the Fertit farms and living in peace and harmony with the Fertit. The Jur Shatt immigrated to the Fertit land as a result of the Jieng mistreating them in their original location.

Unfortunately, during the SPLA aggressions against the Fertit ethnic groups around Mboro, Baggari, and Deim Zubeir, some elements from Jur Shatt joined and supported the SPLA, specifically during their raids on Fertit villages. The SPLA soldiers lacked knowledge about the WBG areas, and the Jur Shatt directed the SPLA units to Fertit houses, farms, and properties.

Some Luo and Fertit tribal leaders, including some elements from the Luo subtribe Jur Shatt, confirmed that some of the Jur Shatt indeed participated in raids on other villages in the Fertit area, including Deim Zubeir. Jur Shatt participation in violence raids against Fertit villages in the south-west of the WBG region created tension between Fertit ethnic groups and the Jur Shatt.

Some inhabitants of Wadhalelo and Kiyango area, who were from the Luo subtribe Jur Abongo, were living in peace and harmony with their neighbours, the Fertit subtribe Balanda, in Kpaile. Unfortunately, after collaboration with the SPLA soldiers, the Jur Abongo attacked the villages around Kpaile.

Later, as the Fertit militia began to function militarily, some Fertit militia leaders chose to attack the positions of the SPLA units, both Jur Abongo and Jur Shatt villages, as a punishment for their participation in the SPLA attacks. The Jur Shatt, who inhabited these villages, fled the area. Many Jur Shatt eventually moved to SPLA-controlled territories and chose to join the movement.

Around Wau County

The formation of the Fertit militia around Wau was different than around Raja. In the villages surrounding Wau, following the first period of violence around the town, Fertit leaders continuously approached the governor of Bahr el Ghazal, Dr Lawrence Wol Wol, for protection. Unfortunately, the governor, a Jieng, allegedly refused to protect the innocent civilians. Instead, he ordered government security forces to withdraw from the Fertit villages, leaving the unarmed Fertit civilians vulnerable to SPLA attacks.

Approaching the governor was the last attempt by Fertit leaders in their search for a lasting solution to bring stability to their villages. The Fertit leaders then developed a plan to turn the already existing organised youth, with white weapons and small arms, into a militia, the Qwat Salam. In order to develop relations with the Sudanese army, Fertit leaders invited Al Tom Al Nur to be overall commander of this forces.

Given the situation in Raja, the Fertit leaders encouraged the civilians who owned guns to bring or use their guns. Those Fertit who were in the military and in security forces in and around Wau they started to abandon their posts and join the militia with their guns. This move by Fertit military men inside the city led to further escalation between the Jieng and the Fertit inside Wau.

Al Tom Al Nur, or Tom Al Nur as the Fertit call him, was an official in Wau. He had a Fertit father from the Fertit subtribe Ndogo, and his mother was of Arab descent from Northern Sudan. Being a mixed-race person qualified Al Tom Al Nur to develop a good relationship between the military officers in Wau and the Fertit militia, who were mostly Christian. This brokerage potential appeared to be the reason why Al Tom Al Nur was asked to command the Fertit militia.

The establishment of the Fertit militia was successful in the first stage. Unfortunately, as the Fertit militia began to function well, some Fertit leaders were unhappy with militia operations in and around Wau, even though it had successfully implemented the task of protecting vulnerable Fertit civilians and their properties from SPLA attacks. These Fertit members feared a dangerous escalation of the war between the two ethnic groups. Further, they distanced themselves from the Qwat Salam because they distrusted those chosen to be militia leaders.

After the formation of the militia forces by Fertit leaders and successfully protecting their villages from SPLA aggressions, the conflict between Jieng militia and Fertit militia escalated inside Wau. According to many witnesses, Wau entered into a state of chaos. Supported by the government, the Fertit militia attacked the Jieng inside the city, particularly the police force named Nyigat.

In the other side, the Jiengs in Wau formed their militia, called Jieng Death Squads, in order to protect themselves from Fertit attacks and counterattacks. Some of the Jieng Death Squads reportedly incorporated personnel from the government security forces, represented by Jieng elements in police, the Wildlife Department, and the Prisons Service. These squads were implicated in killing Fertit civilians and militia members alike. A spiral of violence emerged, resulting in many innocent civilian deaths on both sides.

To stop the cycle of violent in Wau, in late 1988 a local peace agreement was signed between Jieng and Fertit leaders. The agreement involved offering reconciliation and forgiveness from both sides, thereby returning the Fertit militiamen to their normal lives in the community, as well as an equitable distribution of administrative posts in Wau between Jieng and Fertit. However, after the agreement took place, mistrust continued.

CHAPTER 6

FERTIT MILITIA AS COUNTERINSURGENCY

The support of local population is very important for insurgencies around the world to survive in any war. The local population can be a source of information and insurgent reinforcement with food. Unfortunately, by instigating aggressions against the Fertit civilians, the SPLA lost the necessary support from the local Fertit population. Instead, they were chased out of the area by organised local forces.

The Sudanese government capitalised on this opportunity of the SPLA losing the support of the local population. The government in the North made a concerted effort to gain the support of the Fertit civilians in order to militarily win its war with the Sudan People's Liberation Army (SPLA), led by Dr John Garang. Initially, Fertit militia activities concentrated exclusively on the environs of Wau. However, after the militia forces secured the villages from the SPLA units around Wau and Raja, close relations were developed between the Fertit militia and the army in Wau. This relationship developed to military cooperation after the arrival of Major General Abu Gurun Abdullah Abu Gurun, who was redeployed by higher military command in Khartoum to lead government military forces in the town.

The arrival of Abu Gurun Abdullah Abu Gurun in July 1987 involved a large number of reinforcements from Khartoum. These reinforcements included the well-known 242nd Battalion under the command of General Abu Gurun himself.

The beginning of cooperation between the new military commander and the leader of Fertit militia in July 1987 allowed the Fertit militia to undertake large-scale military operations in and around Wau. For instance, in October 1987, the Fertit militia used a military tank to attack the Jieng-controlled police headquarters. With the cooperation of government forces, the Fertit then chased the SPLA completely out of their villages around Raja and Wau.

The wide use of tribal militias as counterinsurgency forces has been implemented by the Khartoum government not only in Wau but also in the all Southern parts of Sudan. By employing militias, the government in Khartoum was able to reduce the need for recruitment of counterinsurgent fighters in the north. Moreover, by using local militias, it allowed the government to deny that there was a civil war in the Sudan at all, as a propaganda argument that the war in the South was really a product of internal Southern tribalism and therefore unrelated to national policies. The policy of supporting tribal militias was not new in the country. The strategy had been used during the first civil war and went back further to the condominium period. Accordingly, there was historical continuity.

In fact, at a minimum, local Fertit actors had a significant role in militia formation. The role of the state became quite important after formation. But even then, there was ambivalence about government support in relation both to the Fertit and to other counterinsurgency tribal militias in the country.

CHAPTER 7

CONCLUSION

Initial SPLA violence against the Fertit might have been an outcome of some undisciplined soldiers among the SPLA units. However, as a result of the tension that emerged after the Torit Mutiny and the ethnic violence in Kordofan before the war in 1983, these events could be another reason for the SPLA forces to attack Fertit villages.

As for the purpose of securing grazing land, throughout the late 1970s and with increasing occurrence during the early 1980s, armed Baggara Arabs, mainly Misseriya, systematically raided Jieng villages with the intent of driving the Jieng out of Kordofan and into the Bahr el Ghazal area.

Some Fertit ethnic groups are related to or considered part of the Baggara. As a result, the SPLA soldiers (predominantly from the Jieng tribe) who were been redeployed around Raja and Wau used the opportunity to seek vengeance by attacking the Fertit in these two areas.

There is no much reason to believe that the SPLA violence in Raja County in 1985 and 1986 was a response to aggression by Fertit from Raja or Wau. There were no intertribal conflict between Jieng and Fertit around Raja. Also, there was no militia formation prior to the arrival of the SPLA in the both Raja and Wau.

In the rural villages of Raja County, there was no build-up of tensions between Jieng and Fertit. By that time, the Jieng community lived relatively far away from Fertit villages, from where the Fertit militia forces emerged.

The only fact that remains constant is the timing of militia formation in Wau, which suggests that the violent instigated by the SPLA against unarmed Fertit civilians had a significant impact on the formation of Fertit militia. That rejected the implicit assumption that the central government had a role in the Fertit militia's formation. The raping and killing of innocent Fertit civilians, as well as the looting of their properties, by the SPLA around both Raja and Wau forced Fertit leaders to organise their own people in order to protect themselves against SPLA aggression.

The life of the Fertit was threatened by the SPLA soldiers who violated Fertit's right to live in peace on their own land. In light of the SPLA attacks on Fertit villages, in order to survive, the Fertit ethnic groups had to organise themselves into militia forces to protect their lives, properties, and villages.

However, after the formation of the militia, the central government turned the event to its advantage. Other Southern communities who experienced SPLA violence during the mid-1980s, especially in the Greater Equatoria region and Jieng land, formed their militias to defend themselves, as the Fertit did.

PART 2

RECAP ON THE JIENG'S FUTURE PLANS

Since a local peace agreement was signed between Jieng and Fertit leaders in 1988, due to common interests against the government in Northern Sudan, there had been no major conflict between the two communities. In general, the relationship amongst the ethnic groups in the Republic of the South Sudan remained relatively calm, except for a few incidents, until the independence of the country.

What followed after the Comprehensive Peace Agreement (CPA) in the Republic of South Sudan (RSS), and particularly in the WBG region, was what Jieng tribal leaders had been planning for in the 1980s and the 2000s. The SPLA aggressions in the region were simply a hangover of the 1980s and a cycle of revenge towards people of the WBG in general and the Fertit community in particular.

At the time when the Republic of South Sudan was going to gain its independence, the SPLM/A did not have a national agenda for the whole country. Instead, the leadership of the SPLM/A had only a hostile agenda favouring their tribe, the Jieng. These tribal agendas included forcefully occupying Fertit land in the WBG region.

Starting in the early 2000s, members of both the Jieng Council of Elders (JCE) and the SPLM/A (predominantly members of the Jieng tribe) were planning for agendas that were advantageous to only their own tribe, and they would implement them after independence. It could be easily be traced back to some events where the Jieng leaders accidentally expressed their intention to instigate violence against Fertit ethnic groups in the future. In the early 2000s, there were few important plans that the Jieng leaders had made to be implemented immediately after the signing of the CPA in 2005, between the government of Sudan and the SPLM/A. On several occasions, the Jieng elites mentioned some details about their hidden plans, which aimed to chase Fertit ethnic groups away from the WBG region to the Central Africa Republic (CAR).

First, in late 2002 and early 2003, Jieng tribal leaders clearly expressed their ill intentions against Fertit groups in an SPLM/A meeting in Rumbek area. In that SPLM/A meeting, chairman and commander-in-chief Dr John Garang de Mabior was present, and some Jieng tribal leaders expressed their future plan to take revenge, displace Fertit ethnic groups from their land, and force them to immigrate to the Central Africa Republic. However, Dr John Garang did not allow deliberation on the issue during that meeting.

Second, in a Mapel meeting during 2004, although the meeting was planned for reconciliation among the Fertit, Jieng, and Luo, the discussion was heated by Jieng radical leaders, who could not hide their anger and future agenda. They expressed a lot of ill feelings against the Fertit. Some SPLM/A Jieng leaders had been waiting for the right time to wage a war of revenge against the Fertit ethnic groups.

Third, in 2008 the Jieng Council of Elders made a master plan, which they called the Dinka Development Plan (DDP), for the next two hundred years. In their plan, the member of the JCE planned for how to rule and dominate other tribes in the Republic of South Sudan. It is very important for the people of the South Sudan to go through this master plan in order to understand why Jieng violently attack other ethnic groups in the country, especially WBG region.

Causes of Conflicts in WBG after the CPA

Immediately after the signing of the Comprehensive Peace Agreement (CPA) between the government of the Sudan and the Sudan People's Liberation Movement and Army (SPLM/A) on 9 January 2005, the Southern part of Sudan, per the Angelo-Egyptian border of 1956, had autonomy. The leadership of the SPLM/A then had political and military control over the Southern part. The SPLM became the ruling party, and the SPLA was absorbed to be the official army and other security forces in the autonomy.

However, in order for the Southerners to win the referendum, there were several reconciliation conferences going on all over the Southern part of Sudan. The leadership of SPLM/A organised a peace conference amongst the ethnic groups of Western Bahr el Ghazal State (WBGS). The conference was organised in Mapel of Jur River County in order for the ethnic groups Fertit, Jieng, and Luo to reconcile and forget the bitterness of the past. All three ethnic groups actively participated and deliberated on the causes of interethnic conflicts. During the deliberations, which lasted for ten days, the communities agreed to reconcile and forgive each other for the sake of peaceful coexistence in the whole WBGS.

Unfortunately, although the reconciliation process took place in Mapel, tensions started to build up again between the Jieng and the Fertit. The high leadership of the SPLM/A, including the president of the republic, Salva Kiir Mayardit, was predominately from Jieng ethnicity, and the Jieng automatically became higher authorities in both political and military posts all over Southern Sudan during the autonomy. Jieng were dominant in political and military posts, and they began to abuse their power. The Jieng elites undermined the rule of law and committed violations against the Fertit community by grabbing land, intimidating Fertit citizens, and physically abusing others in the WBG region.

Tribalism has played a big role in the Southern part of the Sudan, and unfortunately the majority of intellectual Jieng were silent on the Jieng elites' abuses. Therefore the majority of the South Sudanese people sometimes accused the Jieng tribe as being the cause of their suffering, because the Jieng elites damaged the reputation of their ordinary members.

Jieng leaders then had the upper hand in the country and started to smoothly implement their plans of domination of public posts in the WBG region, marginalisation and destabilisation of Fertit, and land grabbing. This was followed by the intimidation of Fertit in Wau.

The period of autonomy was characterised by high rates of intimidation, discrimination, and marginalisation against the Fertit community. Moreover, the Jieng elites began scrambling for Wau land grabs and encroachment of their cattle on farmlands. These were the main causes for the renewal of ethnic tensions in WGBS, particularly in Wau.

Earlier Inhabitants of Wau City

Since the 1800s, the Wau area was inhabited by a host of scattered, disorganised, and diverse Luo and Fertit ethnic groups. The city was an important centre for slave traders.

The Fertit groups in Wau today consider themselves indigenous inhabitants of the city. The Jieng misinterpreted the claim and accused the Fertit community of attempting to chase Jieng tribes out of Wau.

The Jieng, who increasingly immigrated from neighbouring cities after the Fertit groups inhabited the area, were just beginning to dominate, and they continued to maintain their political and economic control over the city. Members of the Jieng community were always ready to defend their positions of domination by all means, including violence.

As the population of Wau scattered, the Jieng first resided in the city without violence from the Fertit or the Luo, the earlier inhabitants in the city. The Jieng have taken advantages of the Fertit and Luo communities being generous and allowing the Jieng to maintain their presence in the city. Fertit ethnic groups have been known for their welcoming spirit and coexisting with other communities who arrived to live in Wau. The welcoming spirit of the Fertit community led to the Jieng, who emigrated from neighbouring states, to implement a policy of domination in the city.

Going back earlier in history, the name Wau did not exist throughout the eighteenth century. The area was called different names. However, the Fertit group lived in the area, which became later the WBG region, and were on the move because of external threats such as slavery. The WBG region became an important slave centre, and by then part of Wau was named Zariba during the Turco-Egyptian rule between 1821 and 1885.

At the first stage of the city's existence, Wau was divided into many small parts near the centre of the current town. At the time when the French were in the city for six months, in 1897 infantry Captain Jean Baptist Marchand, who was a French general, arrived in the area and found the scattered Fertit population in and around what is now the centre of Wau. The French general asked a Fertit tribal chief, Great Bringi, who was from the subtribe Balanda, in order to get approval to establish his headquarters in Wau. The Fertit chief granted permission. After the general received the blessing from the chief, he founded his headquarters on land currently considered to be the centre of Wau, where public buildings, including Parliament and the Peace Hall at the Council of Ministers, were built.

Also, the Luo tribe was considered to be amongst the earliest settlers of Wau. Before the Jieng named Wau, the city was originally named by a local Luo subtribe (Jur Choll) as Geu, which meant *town* in their language. The Luo tribe also called the River Jur as *Gari* or *Gadi*; the Fertit subtribe Bongo was the first to call it *Gedi*. *Gedi* was also used by Fertit subtribes Balanda and Ndogo, who spelled it almost the same as the Bongo, *Ge di*.

The latest arrival was the Jieng tribe, who were accompanied by their leader, Wol Agit. In their migration from the south-east, the Jieng crossed the Jur River and settled north of the River Geti. Chief Wol Agit established friendship with the local Luo chief, Kwany Thyol. The friendship later became complicated until the death of Wol Agit. Wol Agit's son, Agon, moved south of the Gete and settled by Oblong Lake, which is a branch of the Jur River, and they first named this part as Wau.

Jieng had a tradition. As soon as they occupied new places, they gave them their own names immediately to replace the local names. The Jieng, who were the latest arrival in Wau amongst the three communities, not only used the name *Wau* for both the town proper and the surrounding territory, but they also had a tradition in which they explained its origin and meaning. Quickly, the Jieng began to name other areas and trees as *Wau* as well.

Eventually, the Jieng extended their territories to some parts of Northern and Eastern Bahr el Ghazal. They pushed the Luo subtribe Jur Abongo out of the area in order to occupy Aweil land. Similarly, in Rumbek and Tonj, the Jieng violently forced the Fertit subtribe Bongo to abandon their first inhabited areas.

It is worth mentioning that until 1863, no single writer, trader, or traveller who went through the areas of Bahr el Ghazal mentioned the name *Wau*. All places in the region remained without name or with different names. The name *Wau* was mentioned for the first time by Theodore Heughlin when he described his visit to the area. Heughlin travelled in a western direction amongst the Jieng tribe, and then he moved amongst the Luo. After having crossed the Jur River, he continued westwards and then south. He walked for almost four hours arrived at a small river called Wau. From there, he marched for three hours and reached a village called Wau. From Wau, he went to the west and arrived at Zariba after three hours.

The fact that many places in the area were named also as Wau was confirmed by other travellers and writers. Old maps, such as Heughlin's and Schweinfurt's, which was published between 1869 and 1874, described the area lying between Bussere and Jur River as Wau. Similarly, the lower area of Bussere and the Zariba bore the same name, Wau. Interestingly, most of these names changed from time to time.

However, Wau City became an administrative centre during the time of condominium of Anglo-Egyptian rule in the Republic of Sudan from 1899 to 1955.

Between 2005 and 2011, during the time of autonomy and leading to the independence of the Republic of South Sudan, tensions rose as the debate about who were the original inhabitants of Wau. The debate was amongst the three ethnic groups: Fertit, Luo, and Jieng.

Marginalisation of Fertit People

During the implementation of the Comprehensive Peace Agreement (CPA) signed on 9 January 2005 between the SPLM/A and the government of Sudan, specifically at the time of autonomy in the Southern part of Sudan, the SPLM/A, under the leadership of Salva Kiir Mayardit, embarked on a policy of marginalising the people of Fertit in the WBG region. All administration posts in the Western Bahr el Ghazal State (WBGS) were assigned to noncitizens of the state.

When Western Bahr el Ghazal State was established, the three ethnic groups of the state, Fertit, Luo, and Jieng Marial Baii, agreed to form an inclusive state government with top leadership positions distributed fairly amongst the three communities. Unfortunately, at the time the Republic of South Sudan was ten states and WBG became own state, positions such as director of police, director of prison guards, director of wildlife, director of criminal investigation, and other important public positions in the state were continuously occupied by Jieng Marial Baii and noncitizens of the state, specifically by the Jieng who'd immigrated from neighbouring states.

Although the national government of President Salva Kiir politically allocated the position of governor to some Fertit individuals—for example, to Rizik Zachariah Hassan and Angelo Taban Biajo—the real power remained in the hands of Jieng elites. Those Fertit leaders, who were aligning with the government policies, were being given positions, but unfortunately they were being used by the Jieng against their fellow Fertit.

All the positions in the state's security forces were dominated by members of the Jieng, and the Fertit found themselves marginalised. They found it difficult to publicly voice their concerns, especially for those Fertit who were holding public posts. The reason why Fertit did not express their feelings of rejection was due to their fear of being arrested or losing their jobs.

The Fertit in Wau saw it as a betrayal of the earlier agreement, in which the public positions were to be distributed equally amongst the three communities. Also, it contradicted the idea of decentralisation, where members of neighbouring states should be allocated public offices in their own respected states. Western Bahr el Ghazal State (WBGS) remained the only state where people from other states dominated business opportunities, occupied public positions, and became ministers and Members of Parliament in the state.

Land Grabbing

The Transitional Constitution of the Republic of South Sudan, as amended in 2011, stated that all the land belonged to the local community in the country. Although the laws recognised the ownership of the communities, unfortunately this legal right was greatly undermined by Jieng elites, particularly in the Western Bahr el Ghazal State (WBGS). After the independence of the South Sudan on 9 July 2011, the way lands were distributed by the local government involved corruption, which favoured the Jieng and were of great concern to the Fertit community. A Jieng elite in public office was given more than twenty plots, which was against the land regulations in the country. Jieng from neighbouring states who were not residents of Wau but were in the central government in Juba or in the army (the SPLA), were ordering the minister of physical infrastructures or the director of land to allocate each of them with more than one plot.

This mismanagement of land distribution led to all public spaces within Wau being distributed unlawfully to Jieng politicians and military officers. All lands falling within the seven-kilometre radius of Wau Municipality were surveyed and distributed mostly to people who were not from WBGS and were not residents of Wau. After distributing twenty square metres to ordinary Fertit citizens, the Jieng elites ended up with two hundred square metres of land.

Even the land near the Jur River, which was supposed to be invested, was distributed to the Jieng elites. Also, the large public land near the Wau airport was illegally given to only eleven Jieng and some members of the ruling party, including the wife of the president, Mary Ayen Mayardit.

Furthermore, without transparency, the local government distributed and surveyed the land on the Eastern Bank to be first- and second-class plots, and then the government allocated it mostly to Jieng elites and a few members of the local government. The land owned by some citizens was occupied by SPLA, who were from other states. Lands and houses belonging to railways were also occupied by members of the government forces, the SPLA. The farmlands south of the Nazareth area, which were owned by Lorngaiya, were grabbed by government officials, distributed amongst themselves, and renamed by the state government as New Site.

Threats by Pastoralists Activities

Since 2005, Jieng pastoralists have been increasingly allowed by the local authority to march onto farms of the Fertit. The move created seasonal threats, especially to the Fertit farmers in the WBG region. The encroachments of Jiang cattle into Fertit lands mostly emanated from the pastoralists coming from Gogrial and Tonj. Pastoralist Jieng from these cities have been taking their cattle into Fertit farms, where they destroy the crops. As a result of the great damage to the Fertit farmers' crops, the Fertit farmers intervened to stop the cattle. Unfortunately, the farmers were beaten or killed by armed pastoralists. This has created animosity between the cattle keepers and local farmers.

Francis Dongo is a Fertit man who was transferred from Wau to the Agok area to head the wildlife forces. Mr Dongo owned a farm in the area, and some pastoralists came into his farm; their cattle ate and destroyed entire crops. When Francis Dongo failed to stop the pastoralists from entering the farm, he tried to chase the cattle out in order to prevent the cattle from eating the crops. Unfortunately, Mr Dongo failed to stop the cattle from destroying his farm. The pastoralists refused to pull their cattle back or prevent them from eating the crops.

Francis Dongo became angry at the cattle's activities, and he took a gun and shot several cattle. After the chaotic situation, he was beaten by the pastoralists and arrested by security forces. Although Mr Dongo's farm was destroyed by the cattle, he was jailed and fined by the court to pay compensation to the pastoralists for shooting their cattle.

My mother also had a similar incident. She was almost beaten by the Jieng pastoralists in the Momoi area. My family owns a farm in the area, and in 2008, my mother was working the farm alone when the pastoralists came with their cattle and began to destroy crops. She tried to prevent them, but they threatened to harm her. She did not argue with them, in order to prevent confrontation. Instead, she called members of the family, who arrived quickly to resolve the issue. When the pastoralist saw youths arrived, they withdrew with their cattle from the farm.

The government force, the SPLA, and the civil authority in the state tend to support the pastoralists' activities against the farmers. Unfortunately, it was a state policy to arm and support all the Jieng pastoralists against the Fertit and Luo farms. The story of cattle destroying Fertit farms without compensation is common. In fact, the court and local authorities did not take under consideration the threats and damages by the pastoralists. Sadly, there have been several cases where Fertit individuals harmed or killed cattle as a result of the animals destroying their farms. Then they were fined or imprisoned, as in the case of Francis Dongo.

The Jieng pastoralists' activities turned into a belligerent practice that posed constant threats to the livelihood of the Fertit farmers every year, particularly between June and October. Fertit famers questioned the motivation of pastoralists to come all the way from Gogrial, Tonj, and

Northern Bahr el Ghazal with their cattle to graze on Wau farms. There were enough water resources in Jieng lands, and therefore enough grazing land existed in their own lands for their cattle. However, the Fertit famers interpreted the move by pastoralists as another way to destabilise them, forcefully chase them away from their own lands, and occupy their state, the Western Bahr el Ghazal State (WBGS).

CHAPTER 2

PROPOSED MOVE OF STATE CAPITAL TO NGO BAGGARI

Ethnic tensions continued to heighten between the Jieng and Fertit communities for different reasons. In 2012, tensions between the Fertit and Jieng community reignited, this time over the local government proposal to relocate the state capital from Wau to the Ngo Baggari. This was when Wau served as both the capital of Western Bahr el Ghazal State (WBGS) and also represented Wau County.

The then governor of WBGS, Rizik Zachariah Hassan, had first proposed the move in a meeting he headed on 23 August 2011. After the governor initiated the proposal, he formed a committee to study the possibility of moving the capital to Ngo Baggari. The committee also would consult the residents of Wau County on the proposal in an attempt to obtain the needed popular support for his project.

However, the committee came up with results that the people of Western Bahr el Ghazal State (WBGS) in general, and the citizens of Wau in particular, strongly rejected the idea of moving the capital to the Ngo Baggari area. The committee further found that the Fertit perceived the proposal as a way to increase Jieng political dominance by pushing the Fertit away from Wau. Also, the Fertit perceived the relocation of the capital as a way to extend Jieng political and military domination in the surrounding areas, especially Baggari.

Some Fertit further believed that the idea of pushing the Fertit away from the city originated from a tribal community called the Jieng Council of Elders (JCE), a group of Jieng who were influential in national decision-making and were often linked to major policy changes that favoured their tribe. The majority of Wau residents also saw the move as a deliberate, forced migration of indigenous citizens by the government in order to replace them with immigrated Jieng citizens from Abyei, Warrab, Aweil, and Rumbek.

All the above reasons were legal arguments on which the Fertit community based their refusal. Although the concerns raised by Fertit community were legitimate, the state authority ignored Fertit opinion and continued to insist on their plan to relocate the capital. The move by local authorities led to a build-up of political and social tension. Although political and social tensions are elements which are instigating violence globally, the Fertit community refused to choose the path of blood and preferred to peacefully express their views.

Protest against the Relocation of the Capital

The idea of relocation of the capital from Wau to Ngo Baggari was proposed by Jieng elites, Jieng senior politicians, and Jieng military officials. The hidden agenda of the relocation was their plan to occupy and dominate Wau, similar to other places where the Jieng community resided. However, this time the Fertit community was vigilant, and they immediately opposed the relocation.

The Fertit community then adopted civilised and peaceful means to express their refusal, starting with a petition signed by 1,317 Fertit intellectuals, including women and youth in Wau. The petition was intended to raise concerns to the governor, as the higher authority in the state.

The Fertit community, referred to sometimes as the Wau community, proposed their earlier suggestion of increasing the number of counties in the Western Bahr el Ghazal State (WBGS) equally with other states.

While the local authority was pushing to go ahead with the relocation plan, on 7 October 2011 activists organised a meeting with their community members in order to explain to the public the reason behind the government's plan to relocate the capital. In the meeting, the activists made it clear to the public that the reason for the relocation of the capital was to marginalise the Fertit community and extend Jieng domination.

Unfortunately, immediately after the meeting, local authorities faced the peaceful refusal of the relocation via the first arrests amongst Fertit activists. The arrested individuals included Ashab Khamis Fahl (who later became a military officer of opposition forces), Chief Joseph Stephan, John Richard Ukelo, Julio Osman Vilario, John Edward, Chief Joseph Ayan, and others.

With these arrests, the local government attempted to silent the Fertit community in order to proceed with the relocation plan. However, the Wau community continued to oppose the relocation of the capital to Ngo Baggari.

On 8 February 2012, the local government called for a meeting between the governor and the activists. In the meeting, the governor threatened the Fertit community with more arrests if the community continued to oppose his plan. However, despite the threats, the position of the Fertit activists remained unchanged.

Unfortunately, on 17 June 2012 the local government arrested several activists in order to put more pressure on the Fertit community to accept relocation of the capital. This time the arrested Fertit activists were Sebit Archangel Yaba, Oliver Vilario Osman, Late Ceaser Ferdinando Gelego, Danasio William Taban, Shahib Hassen Marsal, Nicola Daldom, and others. Still the Fertit community refused the relocation of the capital from Wau to Ngo Baggari. The arrested activists remained in detention for three months without the basic rights of going to court or meeting their lawyers.

Yet despite the clear popular rejection of the plan by the Fertit community, in October 2012 the governor issued a gubernatorial decree to implement moving the capital to Ngo Baggari, leading to significant anger amongst the Fertit community in Wau. Immediately after the decree was issued, Fertit activists organised a public forum in Wau to debate the issue. During the debate, civilians questioned whether the relocation decision had been supported by the state parliament in accordance with the South Sudan Local Governance Act of 2009. When confronted, some members of the state parliament then denied publicly that the state parliament had agreed with the governor on the decision of relocation. Then the governor ordered his security forces to arrest more Fertit youths, and he removed some local Members of Parliament who stood against his decision from their positions. The National Security Service (NSS) also arrested several Members of Parliament, including the speaker, after they were dismissed from their positions.

After several attempts by activists to convince the local authority to reconsider the relocation of the capital, as a sign of protest the activists adopted peaceful strategies, such as blocking roads connecting Wau to other counties and states, in order to force the state government to back down from its decision to relocate the capital.

On 19 October 2012, when the Fertit activists heard that the newly appointed commissioner was heading to Baggari, some activists implemented the first blockade strategy. They blocked Baggari Road in order to prevent the new commissioner from travelling from Wau to Ngo Baggari.

Meetings between the Activists and the Government

After the Fertit activists successfully prevented the commissioner from reaching his destination, the local government then formed a committee headed by Major General Andrea Dominic, the commander of the government forces, the SPLA Fifth Division stationed in Wau, in order to meet with the activists.

On 21 October 2012, the government committee went to Baggari Road, where the activists made the blockade and entered into a serious discussion with the activists. After the discussion, the two sides agreed to the following.

1. The blockade on the Baggari Road would come to an end immediately.
2. The blocked commercial trucks would be allowed to enter to Wau with their products, in order to avoid prices increasing.
3. No further arrests would be made by state security forces.
4. The capital relocation process by the local government would be suspended.
5. The peaceful protests would continue until the disagreement on the relocation issue was resolved.

6. The activists would form a committee in order to start negotiation with the local authority.
7. The two sides agreed for negotiations to begin immediately, on 23 October 2012, in the headquarters of Wau County.

Right after the above agreement was made, the activists formed their committee in order to meet with the local government. The members of the Fertit activist committee were as follows.

1. Dr Anthony Sokoni Zolinde, Chairperson
2. Sebit Archanjelo Yaba, Deputy Chairperson
3. Julio Vilario Osman, Secretary General
4. Cherillo Khalisto Kako, Secretary of Finance
5. Joseph Daniel, Secretary of Information
6. Archanjelo Philip Amato, Member of the Committee
7. Ceasar Ferdinando Gelego, Member of the Committee

The committee was authorised by the Fertit community to negotiate on behalf of them with the state government, in order to demand the state authority meet three important demands. The Fertit community made their first demand: that the governor cancel the relocation of the capital. The second demand was that the commissioner of Wau County be removed. Finally, the community demanded more consultation about the relocation of the capital to Ngo Baggari.

On the other side, the local government formed its own committee to meet with the activists' delegation. Government members of committee were as follows.

1. An adviser for local governance, Colonel Ufesio Kon Ukok, was appointed by the state authority as chairperson
2. An adviser on political affairs, Colonel Anthony Charles Berinde, was deputy chairperson
3. The state Minister of Information, Derick Alfred Uya, was a member of the committee
4. The commander of government forces, SPLA Fifth Division, Major General Andrea Dominic, was a member of the committee

5. The director of National Security Services in the state, Brigadier General Kon Manyel, was a member of the committee
6. An adviser for security affairs in the state government, Colonel Rizik Dominic Samuel, was a member of the committee
7. A Member of Parliament, Peter Andal, was appointed as a member of the committee

Immediately after the formation of the two committees, the activists prepared their demands. They were optimistic that the issue would be settled peacefully because they believed that their demands and rights were legitimate and therefore achievable.

Indeed, the first meeting between the two committees took place on the agreed-upon date, and the first agenda of the meeting focused on the legitimacy of the gubernatorial decree concerning the relocation of the capital. In the meeting, the committee representing the activists argued that the decree issued by the governor to relocate the capital was in conflict with both the Transitional Constitution of the Republic of South Sudan, 2011, and the South Sudan Constitution on Local Governance, 2009. The activists' argument proven right, but the both sides insisted on their points without concessions. As a result, the first meeting failed to achieve any compromise.

The next meeting took place the following day. In that meeting, the government delegation claimed that the decision of the capital relocation had been approved by the local parliament. Then the activist delegations suggested the meeting be adjourned and they reconvene with some local Members of Parliament, in order to debate on how the local Members of Parliament MPs could possibly agree on an unconstitutional decision. The participants agreed to the adjournment, and the new date was set for the next meeting in a different location, specifically at Hai Salam School, with the presence of Members of Parliament.

The two committees met again on 27 October 2012 in the presence of thirteen Members of Parliament. In the meeting, the MPs denied that the local parliament had approved any decision concerning the relocation of the capital. Furthermore, the MPs illustrated that the decision by the state authority to move the capital to Ngo Baggari was unconstitutional, and therefore it clearly violated the Transitional Constitution of the Republic of South Sudan and ignored the right of local citizens. Given that the decision was considered to be unconstitutional, the MPs who were present in the meeting condemned the move by the local government to unconstitutionally relocate the capital, and they demanded that the process of the relocation immediately be cancelled.

After that meeting, the local authority ignored any calls for further meetings in order to peacefully resolve the issue. Instead, the local authority sought other alternatives. The Fertit community continued their pressure by peaceful means, and they began to gather in huge numbers in Freedom Square, known locally as Medan Tareer.

Thereafter, all attempts by the activists to meet again with the government side was turned down by the state authority. The local government could not bring up a new argument in order to convince the activists, and so authorities saw no need to have more meetings and instead proceeded with the relocation process.

On 3 December 2012, the director of National Security Services in Wau, Brigadier Kon Manyel, requested two activists, Dr Anthony Sokoni Zolinde and Sebit Archanjelo (who were the chairperson and deputy chairperson, respectively), come to National Security Local Headquarters in order to discuss the issue of relocation.

In the proposed meeting, the director of the NSS tried to lobby the two activists to support the government's decision. However, his attempts were unsuccessful. Unfortunately, the discussion turned negative, and therefore Brigadier Kon Manyel ordered his troops to arrest the activists.

After the arrest of Dr Anthony Sokoni Zolinde and Sebitt Archanjelo, the Fertit community held an urgent meeting, where they discussed the arrest and decided to resume protests on 4 December 2012, this time by blocking all roads from and into Wau in order to prevent food items reaching the city, until the security apparatus released their colleagues and started serious negotiations with them. Indeed, after the activists started their blockade on the city, the prices of basic commodities skyrocketed.

Several initiatives, including the Bussere Sons Initiative (created by Taban John Go, Guma Suleiman, and Solomon Dandara) and the United Nations Mission in South Sudan UNMISS initiatives, intended to bring the two sides together in order to resume meetings between the government and the activists. Unfortunately, all these mentioned attempts failed.

In a clear escalation step, on 6–7 December 2012 the government turned to a show of forces by deploying a huge number of troops against the unarmed Fertit community. The local government issued a statement, giving the activists twenty-four hours to open all blocked roads, or else the troops would use any and all means to forcefully reopen the roads.

The grievances committed by the Jieng policies from the beginning—represented by unfair distribution of public posts, land grabbing, pastoralist issues, and the relocation of the capital—pushed the Fertit community to initially express its refusal peacefully. But what prompted Fertit ethnic groups to later change from peaceful expressions against the political and social grievance to violent rebellion?

CHAPTER 3

SHOOTING AT PEACEFUL PROTESTERS

In addition to the blocking of the Baggari Road in peaceful protest, on 8 December 2012 the activists, who continued to stand for the Fertit community's rights, also blocked Bussere Road at the Jebel Rabeh area as a further peaceful protest against the arrests and the relocation of the capital. Unfortunately, although some initiatives continued to look for a peaceful resolution on the disagreed issues, the local government decided to suppress the Fertit community and forcefully put an end to the unrest. The government then used military forces with live ammunition in order to break the blockade on the Bussere Road. The government troops, the SPLA, murdered in cold blood two of the activists, who are considered by the Fertit community to be first martyrs. The deceased were Mr Morris Steven Linga and Mr Dominic Paul Ufindi.

Angered by the event at Bussere Road, on Sunday 9 December 2012 the Fertit community in Wau organised a peaceful protest intended to hand a petition to the office of the governor, protesting the killing of their two colleagues. Unfortunately, the government troops again used excessive force and gunned down seven peaceful protesters—Justin Camilo Dayia, Lawrence George Michael, Albino Thomas Lino, Christopher Andrea Messe, Emmanuel Andrea Mario, Philip Morris Charles, and Remejio Mathew Musa—and injured over twenty individuals. Subsequently, the state government accelerated the process of more arrests with the aim of silencing the activists in Wau, in order to forcefully proceed with the relocation of the capital. The critical question was whether the applied mechanism of force would succeed.

Mr Morris Steven Linga

Mr Dominic Paul Ufindi.

Accusations against Fertit Community

Beginning on 6 April 1994 and throughout the period of genocide, Radio Rwanda and Radio Television Libre des Milles Collines (RTLM) were established as the official Hutu government-owned stations and were used by officials in inciting genocide against Tutsi and moderate Hutu ethnic groups. As in Rwanda, when the radio was used to instigate violence against the rival ethnic group, the officials in Western Bahr el Ghazal State (WBGS) used the local radio to incite hatred and violence against the Fertit groups. Local radio played a significant role in the tragic events in Wau.

Going back to the Rwanda, from October 1993 to late 1994, Hutu leaders used RTLM to advance an extremist Hutu message and anti-Tutsi disinformation, spreading fear of a Tutsi genocide against Hutu, identifying specific Tutsi areas where they could be found, and encouraging the Hutu to commit genocide against Tutsi. In April 1994, Radio Rwanda began to advance a similar message, speaking for the national authorities, issuing directives on how and where to kill Tutsis, and congratulating those who had already done so.

Similarly to the Rwandan style, after the tragic events of 8–9 December 2012, some of the local government officials in Wau, including the governor, intentionally inflamed the already existing, volatile situation by talking on the radio against the Fertit group, particularly the Balanda ethnicity, accusing them of establishing militia and killing Jieng elements. Their speeches on the radio encouraged citizens of the neighbouring states (Warrab, Aweil, and Rumbek) to come in large numbers into Wau, join with those who were already in the city, and take revenge by killing and looting the Fertit.

Also, on 15 December 2012, following the shooting at peaceful protesters, the local government officials, particularly local authorities, went on the on radio to accuse the peaceful protesters of being armed.

On 17 December 2012, Rizik Dominic, the adviser on security affairs in the state, on local radio accused the Fertit subtribe Balanda of killing six Jieng (whom the local official claimed were working as farm workers) in the Farajallah area. The accusation by Rizik Dominic heightened the tension and triggered immediate revenge attacks by Jieng youths on the Fertit neighbourhoods Hai Fahl, Hai Falata, Hai Kalifario, Hai Kresh, and Hai Zande, amongst other areas in Wau. As a result of Jieng attacks, seven Fertit civilians were killed, many more were injured, and over four hundred Fertit homes were destroyed. The revenge aggression by the Jieng against the Fertit community was with the support of local security forces, who were predominantly Jieng.

Unfortunately, on 18–19 December 2012, the killing and looting of Fertit properties intensified in Wau with the help of security forces in the state. During these two days, armed Jieng militia, who'd just arrived in Wau from neighbouring states Warrab and Rumbek, looted Fertit properties, killed twenty-four (including Isa Bandas Aburas, Natale Ireneo Ufo, Alfadel Andal Wedeltala, John Peter Basayo, Aku Jagago, Peter Michael Ukelo, Musa Salah Abdurrahman, Edward Uku, and Philip Atanasio), and injured sixty innocent Fertit civilians.

Additionally, in January 2013, in the weeks following the deaths of six Jieng in the Farajallah area, police and officers from the National Security Service arrested over one hundred civil servants from Fertit. These arrested individuals included youths, politicians, civil society actors, community members, media workers, academics, and members of the police, prison services, and fire brigade. The arrested were accused of failing to stop the protest or of acting in support of the protesters who blocked the roads. According to a Human Rights Report in 2013, because all of those arrested were Fertit, ethnic tensions heightened in the town.

The effect of the radio in Africa evolved rapidly over decades of development. After communication became largely oral, radio broadcasts brought major changes by quickly extending messages. In the South Sudan, radio has been the fastest and easiest way of communication by all stakeholders in the country.

However, the Fertit community believed that the six dead bodies found in the Farajallah area were brought into the area by security forces. In this regard, some Fertit stated that the incident at Farajallah, and subsequent rumours regarding the mutilation of the bodies and more murders of Jieng by the Fertit in the Farajallah area, were fabricated by local authorities in Wau in order to justify the killing of Fertit civilians and the Jieng revenge attacks on the Fertit community, as well as further silencing opposition to moving the capital to Ngo Baggari.

The End of False Accusation

Immediately after the shooting of peaceful protestors by government forces, on 9 December 2012 the SPLA and local government officials justified the shooting by claiming that the protestors were armed and were trying to break into the bank. The Fertit community strongly denied the accusation.

On 16 December 2012 a video clip shown on Al Jazeera news television proved that the protestors were unarmed. The video showed peaceful demonstrators being shot at by the government forces. The video clearly showed that there were no armed individuals amongst the protestors. Instead, the protestors were holding leaves. Al Jazeera reporter Anna Cavell has described the incident live on Al Jazeera: "Having received Al Jazeera new pictures of what appears to be South Sudanese soldiers firing on a crowd of unarmed demonstrators in Wau."

The video was captured by Michael Unjede, one of the activists who had been documenting most of the events in Wau. Right after the tragic event of 8 December 2012, I called Michael on the phone, and he told me that although they were blocking Bussere Road, the government troops removed them by force and killed two activists. Michael further explained to me that they were in the process of writing a petition to be handed to the governor on the following day.

I called Michael again on 9 December 2012, and he was in a chaotic situation, capturing footage while running from the bullets. That was during the shooting at peaceful protestors. Although it was a chaotic situation, Michael Unjede managed to capture the event. He told me that he got pictures of several dead protestor bodies. Michael agreed to hide the video and hand it over to the media. That action saved the reputation of the protestors because the government was later claimed that the protestors were armed.

The President's Visit to Wau

While the Fertit community was going through grief for their losses and the city was still in high tensions between Jieng and Fertit, on 24 December 2012 the president of the Republic of South Sudan, Salva Kiir Mayardit, made an important visit to Wau. The people of Wau were expecting the president to act as a leader for all South Sudanese, interfere in order to lower the tensions, and speak the truth.

Unfortunately, the president did not apologise on behalf of the government forces for shooting at the peaceful protestors. Instead, he endorsed the killing of innocent and unarmed protestors, supported the governor's actions against the activists, and chose to stand with his own tribe, the Jieng, against Fertit ethnic groups. The president publicly announced his support of the killing of peaceful protestors, which had happened earlier.

While addressing the crowd in the stadium, the president threatened the Fertit community, saying, "You cannot handle the problem that you are looking for. If I was here, I would have waged war against you by myself. The destruction is not difficult, and a city like Wau could be destroyed in two hours only." Immediately after what could be considered hate speech against an ethnic minority, the security forces in the city embarked on more arrests of Fertit civilians, and the tragic situation escalated to worse levels.

After these events, many Fertit youths fled to areas surrounding Wau, fearing arrest and reprisal. Eventually, these youths voluntarily joined the Fertit Lion Forces at the first stage.

The killing of civilians by the government forces, the SPLA, was not new. There were similar incidents all over the country. For example, in 2009 the SPLA killed Shilluk civilians in Malakal, followed by the murdering of Murle civilians in 2010, because of the rebellion by David Yao Yao, one of the Murle leaders. The Wau incident in 2012 was the tip of the iceberg; the SPA eventually went house to house, killing Nuer civilians during the power struggles in 2013.

CHAPTER 4

FORMATION OF THE FERTIT INSURGENCE

Grievances, marginalisation, land grabbing, suppression, social tension, critical events, and many causes were the reasons why the Fertit community in the Republic of South Sudan developed insurgent forces. Ideological, social, and economic tensions prompted Fertit leaders to rally for their insurgent foundation. These are the fundamental issues that engaged the hearts and minds of the Fertit population and motivated them to become insurgents.

The national government, under the leadership of President Salva Kiir Mayardit, continued to pressure local authorities to suppress the Fertit community. This resulted in the local authority suspending more than nine Fertit Members of Parliament, who were accused of supporting protests against the relocation of the capital. The pressure by the regime in Juba let the security forces arrest and commit violence against Fertit civilians in Wau. In the aftermath of the arrests, tensions continued to simmer. These tensions were then escalated by the sentences handed down by a special court made up of three judges who had been sent from Juba. The judges were brought in to investigate the Farajallah issues and other events that had led to the arrests of activist. The special court accused a total of eleven Fertit youths, who were then sentenced to death by hanging.

However, some Fertit activists who were been arrested (including the chief of Farajallah) received less punishment. The chief was sentenced to ten years in prison, and three Members of Parliament (John Richard

Ukelo, Julio Venansio Mango, and Angelo Marcilo Fak) were found guilty of organising protests against the transfer of the Wau County headquarters to Ngo Baggari. Those MPs were sent to Wau's prison to serve two-year prison terms. Other youths were given prison sentences as well.

In the light of the Fertit community being suppressed by government troops, the SPLA (predominantly Jieng), arbitrarily committed arrests, tortures, lootings, and killings against the innocent Fertit civilians in Wau. The Fertit community therefore felt like there was an urgent need to be freed from the difficult situation. Consequently, the peaceful protest from activists turned to violence. The people of Western Bahr el Ghazal State (WBGS) secretly established a foundation for the Fertit Lion Forces, which later changed its name to Western Bahr el Ghazal Lion Forces (WBGLF).

The establishment of the Fertit Lion Forces aimed to defend themselves against the threats of the government's troops and its militias, both of which were predominately Jieng. For the second time in their history, the Fertit had to wage a war of destiny against the Jieng, who committed human rights violations and crimes. The move by the Fertit to quickly organise their forces prevented, for the second time in their history, a Rwandan genocide from happening. In which they avert atrocity that was planned by Jieng elites against them.

This marked the second time in the history that, as in the Anya-Nya I, the Fertit were the first amongst the people of the South Sudan to fight dictatorship tendencies under President Salva Kiir, demanding federalism, equality, justice, and democracy.

Opposition to the government in the WBG region was rooted in a perception amongst the Fertit community that members of the ruling party and its army wing, the SPLM/A, were indeed implementing a Jieng plan in order for them to seize power and take control of Fertit land, as well as business opportunities and public positions. This decades-old perception was born out of several events during the First and Second Sudanese Civil Wars, from 1955 to 1972 and from 1983 to 2005, respectively. The civil wars took place between the Anya-Nya I and the government in the North, and the government of Sudan and the Sudan People's Liberation Movement/Army SPLM/A under the leadership of late John Garang de Mabior.

For the Fertit, the fear of Jieng dominance was reinforced by the events that followed the period of 2006–2011, particularly the events of the moving of the Wau County capital to Ngo Baggari. These events encouraged them to form their opposition forces. Additional issues forced the Fertit groups to mobilise an armed resistance, which was related to the tensions between the Fertit and the Jieng over the movements of the Jieng pastoralists' cattle, aggressions by government forces against Fertit, the immigration of the Jieng to Wau, and lastly the annexation of Fertit land in the WBG region through the creation of twenty-eight new states in South Sudan since 2015.

CHAPTER 5

CONCLUSION

The Fertit community in the Western Bahr Ghazal region has gone through marginalisation and domination by Jieng leaders. Government forces (predominantly Jieng) have violently targeted the Fertit community in order to occupy the region. These Jieng attempts to dominate the Fertit community were why political and social tensions built up in the region. That initially led the Fertit community to peacefully express its anger.

In order to address the tensions in the region, the government should have swiftly addressed the concerns raised by the Fertit community. The government needed to understand the historical proclivities behind the Fertit refusal of the illegal relocation of the capital to Ngo Baggari. The government should have immediately addressed the legitimate concerns of Fertit community, as well as halted discrimination against the Fertit community and the economic exploitation of the WBG region. Unfortunately, the government attempted to suppress the Fertit community.

The unfair treatment led to political and social tension for the Fertit community during Rizik Zachariah Hassan's term, and the tactics are being used globally by other groups to form and develop rebellions against governments.

The Fertit community felt violently suppressed and mistreated; their future became uncertain, and they became victims of Jieng oppressors. Therefore they decide to take charge of their destiny by rebelling against the marginalisation, mistreatment, intimidation, suppression, abuses, and violence by the government forces, the SPLA and Mathiang Anyor (predominantly Jieng), under President Salva Kiir Mayardit.

PART 3

CHAPTER 1

THE FORMATION OF THE SPLM/A-IO

The Rise of Disagreement within SPLM

After many disagreements amongst the political and military leaders in the Southern part of Sudan, in order to be united during the peace negotiations with the government in the North, the Nairobi Declaration was achieved in 2002. The leadership of the SPLM/A, under the chairmanship of Dr John Garang de Mabior, initiated a process of reconciliation with other Southern opposition parties before signing the Comprehensive Peace Agreement (CPA) with the government in the North on 9 January 2005.

The Nairobi Agreement aimed to reconcile and create unity amongst South Sudanese, in which Dr Riek Machar rejoined the SPLM/A as a senior commander. Unfortunately, the reconciliation was aimed only to unite the people of the Southern part in order to win the upcoming referendum. By then, Jieng tribal leaders needed the Southern people to win the referendum.

The CPA was meant to end the Second Sudanese Civil War, establish a Government of National Unity (GONU), and share oil revenues between the government in the North and the Government of South Sudan (GOSS) in its autonomy.

Dr John Garang served as the chairman of the SPLM/A, was the first vice president of Sudan, and was the president of Southern autonomy during the first stage of implementation of the CPA. He briefly served from 9 July 2005 until his death in a helicopter crash near New Site on 30 July

2005. Dr John Garang was a great leader of the SPLM/A, and he led the struggle for the foundation of a new Sudan based on democracy, equality, rule of law, and separation of religion from the state.

General Salva Kiir Mayardit was Dr John Garang's deputy. General Kiir eventually rose to be the chairman of the SPLM/A and the head of Southern autonomy, and on 11 August 2005 he was sworn in as the first vice president of Sudan. Dr Riek Machar replaced Salva Kiir as deputy chairman of the SPLM/A.

The party lost its vision after the loss of its leader, and therefore the SPLM/A had to organise itself and upgrade new leaders. Leaders of the party proposed national conventions to be held later, where they could nominate candidates, establish a party platform, and rally their members for campaigns in preparation for the upcoming election. In the proposed national convention, besides taking care of party's official business (such as democratically electing party leaders for the first time and developing the SPLM/A's Internal Regulation on key issues heading into elections), the members of the party also could come together in one place for first time since the first convention in 1994.

The SPLM's first national convention was held in 1994 at the time of the Sudanese Civil War, in a secret place and under the threat of aerial bombardment from the regime in Khartoum. The second convention brought together more than one thousand five hundred delegates from all Sudanese states, as well as many from the Diaspora. The attendants represented the different religions and ethnic groups that make up Sudan. The national convention was held in the auditorium of Juba's brand-new Cultural Centre, Nyakuron Centre.

The anger to power led to the disagreement amongst the members during the second national convention of the SPLM in May 2008 regarding the position of the chairman of the party. Few leaders, including Dr Riek Machar Teny and Nhial Deng Nhial, have showed their aspirations for the post of chairmanship, which Salva Kiir serviced without any intention of relinquishing power, since the death of Dr John Garang. The presence of Salva Kiir on top of the government was seen by the Jieng elites as a golden chance to implement their tribal plan that favoured the Jieng. Salva Kiir represented hope for many tribal Jieng leaders due to his readiness to implement their tribal agenda without hesitation. Therefore, Salva Kiir wanted to continue as the chairman of the SPLM/A and the first vice president of the Sudan.

However, efforts by the leaders of the SPLM/A to resolve the leadership issue led to the situation amongst the SPLM leadership to be cooled down, in order for the party to focus on the referendum that took place in Southern part of the Sudan from 9 to 15 January 2011. The result of the referendum was announced on 7 February 2011, with 98.83 per cent of South Sudanese registered voting in favour of independence from the country. For Jieng elites, the result came as they wished. However, for the people of the country, it was uncertainty but also hope for a better future. The majority of Southerners were happy about the referendum result, in which they would gain their own country.

After the Republic of South Sudan gained its independence, Salva Kiir Mayardit remained the chairman of the party and became the first president of the Republic of South Sudan. Dr Riek Machar Teny Dhurgon continued to serve as deputy chairman of the SPLM/A, and he automatically became the vice president of the republic.

In the first stage, the situation remained the same—until the debate rose again amongst the leaders (President Salva Kiir, Dr Riek Machar, and others) regarding who should be the party's candidate in the next internal election, when the party would elect the next chairman of the movement and therefore the next president. In order to resolve the issue democratically, the leadership of the movement chose to go for an internal election during what was planned to be the third national convention.

A power struggle began amongst the leadership of the SPLM party. Several leaders poured their efforts into becoming the next leader. The senior members of the party continued their call for the national convention, although another disagreement emerged amongst the SPLM/A leaders about how to vote in order to elect the new chairman.

Before the proposed convention, in February 2013 the SPLM Political Bureau held a consultative meeting in order to prepare the party's internal regulations and other issues before presenting it to the members of SPLM National Liberation Council (NLC), to be debated and proved ahead of the third national convention.

In the Political Bureau meeting, the discussion of how to elect the chairman of the SPLM/A in order for their candidate to be the South Sudan president remained without a solution. Then the picture became more complicated, with more high-ranking political leaders of the party wanting to replace their chairman. Dr Riek Machar, Bagan Amom (who was the secretary general of the party), and Robecca Nyandeng de Mabior (the widow of the late Dr John Garang) were amongst the leaders who announced their intention to be candidates for the position. Salva Kiir Mayardit wanted to continue as the SPLM/A chairman and remain as the head of the state.

The members of BP could not agree on how to select the new chairman, and the discussion of how to vote and select the new chairman was adjourned for a month. There would be another meeting with all senior members of the both the Political Bureau and the National Liberation Council in order to agree on the basics of the SPLM constitution, specifically on whether to allow

1. direct vote by raising hands, which was preferred by President Salva Kiir, or
2. a secret ballot, which was preferred by other leaders (including Dr Riek Machar).

The Dismissal of Senior Members

Members were waiting for President Salva Kiir, as the chairman of the SPLM, to call for the suggested third national convention. However, the chairman was avoiding the internal election, leading to the build-up of frustration amongst members of the party.

In May 2013, Dr Riek Machar publicly announced his intention to replace Salva Kiir as the chairman of the SPLM/A party and become the president of the republic. The move by Machar quickened the deterioration of the relationship between Salva Kiir and Riek Machar.

Machar's announcement to contest the chairmanship triggered the president to release him as head of the National Reconciliation Committee and suspend the activities of the committee on 16 April 2013. Furthermore, the president got more aggressive in his efforts to secure his position by issuing two presidential decrees on 23 July 2013, one for releasing Dr Riek

Machar as vice president of the Republic of South Sudan, and another decree for the dismissal of Bagan Amom as SPLM secretary general. The decrees were intended to intimidate Dr Riek Machar and push him to rethink his candidacy.

However, while addressing the press on 25 July 2013, Dr Riek Machar accepted his dismissal, confirming that the president had a constitution right to remove him from the vice president's office.

Although the releasing of Dr Riek and Bagan Amom aimed to intimidate them, the members of the SPLM party (including the two dismissed men) continued to put pressure on Chairman Salva Kiir Mayardit to call for the third national convention, in order to discuss the reform agenda within the party and vote on the SPLM's internal regulation. However, the Chairman continued ignoring calls by the party to invite the members for the meeting.

The Press Conference

In order to exert more pressure on the president to call for the national convention, on 6 December 2013, senior members of the SPLM, who considered themselves reformists and who were represented by Dr Riek Machar, Bagan Amom, Robecca Nyendeng de Mabior, Deng Alor, John Lok, Kosti Manibe, Dr Peter Adok Nyaba, Taban Deng Gai, Ezekiel Lul Gatkuoth, Alfred Lado Kure, and others, held a press conference in the capital, Juba. In the press conference, they illustrated the grassroots that had caused disagreement within the party, as well as the lack of freedom, democracy, accountability, and development in the country. The members of the group further raised their concerns about the dictatorship tendency the country was falling under due to the leadership of President Salva Kiir Mayardit.

They explained to the public the efforts made by them in order to establish reform and bring democratic change within the SPLM/A party (and therefore in the whole country). They talked about members' right to run and hold any position in the party. The press conference ended by announcing a public rally to be held on 14 December 2013.

With this press conference, the power struggle amongst the members of the SPLM party became a public issue and was debated amongst the citizens. The opinion of the South Sudanese people was divided, with the majority supporting the democratic reforms and blaming the president.

After the press conference, it became very clear to Salva Kiir and his followers that the reformists, led by Dr Riek Machar, were serious about their agenda concerning the party's internal election to bring new leadership to the party and the country as a whole. Tension was high in the capital amongst members of the same party, which divided into two groups,

The United Nations Mission in South Sudan (UNMISS), represented by Hilda Jonson, the US ambassador, Suzan Page, and the Catholic Church (represented by Archbishop Paulino Lukudu Loro) tried to defuse the tension. After these efforts and mediation, finally Chairman Salva Kiir agreed to call for a long-awaited NLC conference to be held between 14 and 16 December 2013. It was surprising that Salva Kiir picked the same date that the reformists had announced for a public rally.

The mediators put pressures on the reformists to suspend their rally and participate in the meeting announced by Chairman Salva Kiir. The reformists agreed to postpone their rally and attend the national convention meeting.

In the conference, delegates were expecting the president to lower his tone, call for reconciliation, and accept the internal election. But surprisingly, Salva Kiir made an aggressive speech. That annoyed the mediators, who had put in a lot of effort to resolve the leadership issue amongst SPLM members.

At the opening of the conference, Salva Kiir lashed out at his opponents, and he was quoted as saying, "The freedom that we enjoy today in South Sudan came through difficulties during the SPLM/A struggled between Khartoum Regime and the SPLM/A. Therefore, my leadership will not allowed 1991, referring to an incident which ethnic Jieng has been slaughtered by forces loyal to Riek Machar, to happen again in South Sudan." The president continued by saying, "Some of my friends claims to be historical, but nobody be the historical. The SPLM should not be monopolised by few and therefore, some of my friends challenged me, no one will challenge me again in the history of South Sudan." The situation at the conference became more tense as some members, including the president, began singing a song in the Jieng language.

On the second day of the convention, 15 December 2013, some members of the SPLM political party who called themselves reformists were prevented by government security from attending the meeting. Dr Riek Machar, who was still the deputy chairman of the party, and a few of his colleagues were allowed to enter to the hall. However, Dr Riek Machar wouldn't give his speech that day, which led to members of the reformists who'd made it inside withdrawing from the conference during the break.

Shooting at the Military Barracks

The political situation amongst the members of the SPLM worsened, which caused a warning in the country. The majority of the government forces were tribal, predominantly Nuer and Jieng, so the tribal army had loyalty to their tribal senior members. It was difficult to predict the outcome of this disagreement.

At night on 15 December 2013, shootings started within the presidential guards, known as Tiger Special Forces. The gunfire started after one of the presidential guards, who was a Jieng officer, tried to disarm ethnic Nuer within the presidential guards. This triggered a group of Nuer presidential guards to refuse the disarmament. The clashes occurred in the old military barracks inside the capital and continued for about one hour before one group was expelled.

On 16 December 2016, the government army loyal to President Salva Kiir came with tanks and destroyed the house of Dr Riek Machar, which had more than fifteen guards. The government army killed all guards. They also destroyed the house of Gier Chwong.

The shooting then spread to the capital, Juba, where in one incident, predominantly Jieng security forces from the Gudeli area gathered hundreds of Nuer men during the night of 16 December 2013 and detained them in a building used by the police, near the junction that divides Gudeli One and Gudeli Two. An estimated three hundred Nuer civilians were jammed into a room. Then the government forces shot into the room through windows on one side of the building, killing all of the people in the room.

Witnesses in the capital confirmed the gunfire and blasts were heard throughout the night around the city, and fighting intensified the following morning. The fighting mostly subsided by midday, with witnesses reporting sporadic gunfire in some areas and a heavy military presence in the city.

For his first appearance after the shooting, on 16 December 2013 President Salva Kiir appeared on the South Sudan local television. The president was surrounded by his close ministers and wore combat fatigues instead of his usual civilian clothes. The president fabricated a coup attempt, falsely accusing Dr Riek Machar and his group of attempting to seize power by force. The president immediately declared a curfew. The fabricated coup was an attempt to justify the curfew. The curfew aimed to isolate the Nuer and his opponents, after which his militia went door to door murdering the Nuer civilians.

The issue of leadership within the SPLM party under the chairmanship of President Salva Kiir Mayardit was to blame for the killing of innocent civilians and destroying the country. The disagreement amongst the political officials of the party could have been resolved politically if South Sudan had not lacked political leadership; rather, it had tribal leaders.

Arrests of the Reformists

The accusation by the president against Dr Riek Machar and his colleagues triggered systemic house-to-house arrests, as well as the killing, raping, and torturing of innocent Nuer civilians by security forces loyal to the president. Victims and witnesses told Human Rights Watch that government soldiers of the SPLA, predominantly Jieng, questioned residents about their ethnicity and deliberately shot ethnic Nuer.

Throughout the week, the SPLA, under the command of Jieng Generals Marial Chinoung, Marial Nour, Salva Mathok, Aleu Ayieny Aleu, and Paul Malong Awan, massacred over two thousand innocent Nuers in the capital.

As the government forces targeted Nuer civilians, thousands of people fled their houses in Juba during the first day, including more than sixteen thousand civilians who sought shelter at the compound of the United Nations Mission's protection centres in the capital.

Government forces specifically were trying to arrest all the reformists, including Dr Riek Machar. However, Dr Machar was protected in a hidden place by his bodyguards and remained at large before appearing in Junglei State after more than a month. Similar to the Fertit situation, Dr Riek Machar and his close bodyguards had to run for their lives. Dr Machar then had to form his armed movement, later called the Sudan People's Liberation Movement and Army in Opposition (SPLM/A-IO).

However, most of the reformists were arrested in the capital, Juba. Those arrested on the first day included Oyay Deng Ajak, Gier Chuang Aluong, Majak D' Agot, John Luk Jok, Cirino Hiteng, Kosti Manibe, Deng Alor, Madut Biar, Chol Tong Mayay, and Ezekiel Lul Gatkuoth. This was followed by more arrests in the next following days, including Pagan Amom. After pressure exerted by the Intergovernmental Authority on Development (IGAD), all of the senior members of the party who had been arrested were later released by the government and travelled in exile to the Kenyan capital, Nairobi. Subsequently, the group formed their unarmed resistant movement, which called itself Former Detainees (FDs), under the leadership of Pagan Amom.

The political crisis that led to the clashes in Juba marked the deterioration of security situations across the country; a heightening of tensions between communities of different ethnicities, particularly between the Jieng and the Nuer; and the first civil war after independence.

The inception of the Sudan People's Liberation Movement and Army in Opposition (SPLM/A-IO) came about as a result of President Salva Kiir Mayardit and his administration resisting critical political reforms needed in the country. This led to the unfortunate Juba events that began on 15 December 2013, in which thousands of Nuer were slaughtered in cold blood by government forces.

Subsequently, the Nuer community and the lives of some politicians were threatened by government forces, and the violence spread to other parts of the South Sudan. The situation encouraged the establishment of the SPLM/A-IO, therefore starting civil war in the country.

After the escalation of these events, with the escaping of Dr Riek Machar, several members of SPLM/A, including Dr Riek Machar Teny, were on the move to make an historical decision to separate from the SPLM/A under President Salva Kiir Mayardit. The official declaration of the SPLM/A-IO was made on 17 April 2014 at Nasir Consultative

Conference. The principles of the formation of the SPLM/A-IO were made clear: to defend the people of South Sudan and to establish a federal system of governance in the Republic of South Sudan comprising twenty-one federal states based on the former districts of the Southern provinces of Anglo-Egyptian rule. Raja and Wau would be two separated states, with their borders as they had been on 1 January 1956.

Moreover, the formation of the SPLM/A-IO aimed to foster a political ideology whereby the states played a leading role in the social and economic development of their people. Most South Sudanese citizens of non-Jieng ethnicity, especially people of WBG region, shared the objectives of SPLM/A-IO leadership.

CHAPTER 2

Joining the SPLM/A-IO

The fighting that broke out between the Jieng and Nuer soldiers on 25 April 2014 in the Mapel barracks close to Wau had a direct impact upon the Fertit opposition. Fighting was triggered by Jieng community members attacking Nuer SPLA trainees in a local market.

After the clashes, Nuer SPLA soldiers deserted their posts, fearing further attacks. They moved to Fertit areas, where they were stationed until their departure. This incident marked remarkable cooperation between Fertit and Nuer opposition leaders.

Before the establishment of the SPLM/A-IO, the Fertit Lion Forces fought the government forces, the SPLA, around Raja and Wau. The mobilisation of Fertit Lion forces outside of Wau was inspired by local concerns and the government forces' aggression against Fertit civilians. The Fertit Lions were also heavily influenced by the conflict between the government and the SPLM/A-IO. Fertit opposition leaders realised that some of the Fertit local issues that they were to fight for, such as federalism and equal representation, were related to the wider national agenda that they shared with the leadership of the SPLM/A-IO.

The SPLM/A-IO and the Fertit Lion Forces, had several things in common. Both movements never planned to start a war. Instead, they were pushed to mobilise and organise their people and fight after peacefully demanding their rights and reforms failed.

Secretary General of SPLM/A-IO Tingo Peter (2018)

Several Fertit political and military leaders, including Peter Tingo, Thomas Bazilio Tendo, Ashab Khamis Fahl, and Salah Mamoki, contacted the chairman and the commander-in-chief of the SPLM/A-IO, Dr Riek Machar. An agreement was made in 2014 for the Fertit Lion Forces to form an alliance with the SPLM/A-IO.

Because the people of Western Bahr el Ghazal (WBG) region shared the same principles and objectives with the SPLM-IO, in August 2014 the political and the military leaders of the WBG region made an official declaration of joining the SPLM/A-IO. The political leaders from the WBG region had been assigned political posts, and military commanders of the Fertit Lion Forces were reorganised, promoted, and assigned military missions in their respected regions of Western Bahr el Ghazal (WBG).

The deal was seen to be mutually advantageous. The SPLM/A-IO would be able to expand its representation across the country, use additional garrison sites and other resources, bring another group under its umbrella, and be a nonethnic and inclusive movement, thereby increasing its leverage in future negotiations with the government in Juba.

For the Fertit side, they could realise several fundamental advantages for joining the SPLM/A-IO. First, their demands would be raised through the SPLM/A-IO on the national level, and some of their dream—for instance, having a federal system in the county—would be achieved through the SPLM/A-IO because they would be included in national political negotiations through the Agreement on the Resolution of the Conflict in South Sudan (ARCSS), which was under way at that time, with a federal system of government, reforms, and equal representation as their end goal. Second, they would gain access to resources and military training. The view of national inclusion became important following the presidential decree increasing the number of states in South Sudan from ten to twenty-eight and then thirty-two controversial states.

Indeed, the Fertit Lion Forces became more militarily modern than in 1985, during Qwat Salam. By joining an alliance with the SPLM/A-IO, under the leadership of the chairman and commander-in-chief, Dr Riek Machar, the Fertit and Luo were retrained, promoted with both political and military ranks, restructured, and united.

CHAPTER 3

FROM FERTIT LION FORCES TO WBGLFs

In the first stage of establishing Fertit Lion Forces, few Luo political and military leaders were inspired by and sympathised with the Fertit opposition. They joined the Fertit Lion Forces and therefore were moved into the liberated areas around Wau and Raja. Specifically, in 2015 another group of military and political Luo joined the movement in large numbers. The opposition military activities increased amongst the Luo. In their process to join the opposition forces, some of the Luo contacted Fertit leaders in order to be recruited into the Fertit Lion Forces. Others joined the SPLM/A-IO and were promoted and then given military assignments by the SPLM/A-IO leadership, going back to their respective WBG regions.

In 2015 Simon Udom, Natali Ujok, Valentino Ukeg, and others were amongst the Luo leaders who joined the SPLM/A-IO and travelled to Pagak, the headquarters of SPLM/A-IO by then, in order to receive and acquire the necessary military training. This group played a significant role in recruiting other Luo, and they were considered to be the first to recruit Luo sons and daughters in order to join both the Fertit opposition and the SPLM/A-IO.

With the support of the leadership of both SPLM/A-IO and Fertit, the Luo leaders strengthened their presence around Kuajiena County. The numbers of the SPLM/A-IO troops in Kuajiena were then boosted by the defection of Brigadier General Majok Thual Thual Madut, and they created strong forces, which became part of Sector 7 of WBGLFs.

Governor Brig. Gen. Dayia Ahmed Faraheldor (2017)

Also, in the same year a police brigadier, Andrea Peter, travelled to the liberated areas around Wau with a number of Luo sons in order to join the armed resistance movement. Wildlife officer Majok Thual Thual rebelled from Wau and joined the opposition forces in Baggari. Majok Thual Thual Madut was then promoted to the rank of brigadier general and assigned to lead the Fifth Brigade, stationed around Kuajiena, with his headquarters in Wedhalelo.

The joining of Luo into the opposition forces was the reason why the name of the Fertit Lion Forces was changed to the Western Bahr el Ghazal Lion Forces (WBGLF).

Political Restructure

On 16 July 2014, the SPLM/A-IO, under the leadership of Dr Riek Machar Teny, proposed the creation of twenty-one states for a Federal Republic of South Sudan. When the movement was officially formed, the SPLM/A-IO then began to implement its proposal and divided the South Sudan into twenty-one federal states, with their borders as they had originally stood on 1 January 1965, with Wau and Raja becoming separated states.

After the armed opposition forces of WBG formed an alliance with the SPLM/A-IO under the leadership of Dr Riek Machar Teny, Teny then appointed two governors in opposition in their liberated territories, around Raja and Wau. Tingo Peter Robigo and Brigadier General Dayia Ahmed Faraheldor were appointed to be the governor of Wau and Raja, respectively.

The chairman also appointed Tingo Peter Robigo, Ufindi Dema, Simon Udom Eye, Oliver Valario Osman, Elia Paul Ngori, Gabriel Ungom, Tony Costa Lual, Mohammed Ali Goni, Dayia Ahmed Fraheldor, Peter Marcilo Nasir, Abdullah Rahama, Said Bandas Ezadeen, Sandra Bona Malual, Claudio Francis Omdurman, Suna Musa Juma, and Alhadi Eisa Gardud to be members of the National Liberation Council (NLC) from Raja and Wau.

On 1 December 2016, Dr Riek Machar appointed Tingo Peter as a secretary general of SPLM/A-IO, replacing Dr Dhieu Mathok Diing, who had defected and remained in Juba when violence erupted in July 2016 at presidential palace J1.

On 10 January 2017, the chairman and commander-in-chief of the SPLM/A-IO, Dr Riek Machar, appointed me, with a major general military rank, as military governor in Wau for the opposition, replacing Tingo Peter. Per the constitution of the SPLM/A-IO, as with other governors, I automatically became a member of National Liberation Council. The NLC was considered to be the highest legislative authority in the movement.

On 27 July 2017, Dr Riek Machar Teny Dhurgon, the chairman and commander-in-chief of SPLM/A-IO, appointed major general Salah Momegi Mameri, who was the deputy commander of Sector 7, as a governor of Raja in opposition, replacing Brigadier Dayia Ahmed Faraheldor. Similarly the chairman and commander-in-chief of SPLM/A-IO issued another decree replacing me with my deputy, major general Anthony Fada, as the governor of Wau state in opposition

Governor Maj. Gen. Dominic Ukelo (2017)

The first conflict between Jieng and Fertit in the 1980s was different from the war that started the conflict in 2012. This time, Fertit politicians were deeply involved in mobilising troops and resources, as well as organizing civil authority in the liberated areas controlled by opposition forces, where there was a large number civilians, who fled their homes and sought refuge.

As a Governor, for the first time in the history of the Fertit struggle against the regime, I was able to establish a strong structure of civil authority in the liberated area around Wau. The civil authority under my leadership then formed both civil authority and civil courts to reinforce the rule of law amongst civilians under our control, mobilised resources for the civilians, raised the demands of the region, explained to the media the reason behind our struggle against the government, prepared the demands of our people for the peace negotiation in 2017, and participated in negotiation with the government on behalf of our people.

During the negotiation of the R-ARCSS, all the people of the WBG region contributed ideas. Through the SPLM/A-IO, leaders from WBG region; Elias Nyamlel, Peter Marcilo Nasir, and Lieutenant General Thomas Bazilio Tindo were present in Ethiopian-Addis Ababa.

Military Restructure

At the first stage of the Fertit resistance, the forces were operated without a central command. Each area around Raja and Wau operated separately but in cooperation with each other. One major benefit of forming an alliance in armed opposition with the SPLM/A-IO was unification of command. Further benefits included the unity between Fertit forces and Luo troops under one structure, as well as harmonisation amongst the Western Bahr el Ghazal Lion Forces (WBGLF) around Wau and Raja in order to be stronger under one military command. In order for the SPLM/A-IO leadership to upgrade the Western Bahr el Ghazal Lion Forces, after forming an alliance with the SPLM/A-IO in August 2014, the WBGLF around Raja and Wau were then renamed to Sector 7. Lieutenant General Fayez Ismail Fatur shortly served as the first overall Commander of Sector 7. Lieutenant General Fayez Ismail Fatur had a significant role in setting the foundation, organizing the WBGLF, and creating the headquarters of Sector 7.

Governor Lt. Gen. Salah Mamuki (2018)

When General Fayez was redeployed to the SPLA-IO Council of the Joint Chiefs of Staff, Major General Thomas Bazilio Tindo was promoted to the military rank of lieutenant general, and the chairman and commander-in-chief of SPLM/A-IO appointed him as overall commander of Sector 7.

Major General Salah Momegi Mameri was deployed as deputy commander, Major General Ashab Khamis Fahl was deputy for administration and finance, Major General Peter Pal Gatkuoth was deputy of operation, and Major General Hussein Galla Andal was deputy for logistics. Brigadier General Sharif Mamedo Dali was appointed to chief of the National Security Services and General Intelligence for Sector 7. Most important, Brigadier General Sharif Mamedo Dali had a main role in restructuring the WBGLF concerning the issue of military reinforcement, redeployment, and promotions.

The Western Bahr el Ghazal Sector 7 was divided into two divisions. Division 6A was stationed around Wau, and Division 6B was stationed near Raja. Division 6A was commanded by Major General Abdullah Ujang Ukuon, with Brigadier General Lino Ramadan Gudu as deputy commander, Brigadier General Francis Donga Joseph Ufo as deputy for administration and finance, Brigadier General Emmanuel John Utong as deputy for operation, and Brigadier General Said Darnas Said as deputy for logistics.

Division 6A was divided further into five brigades around Wau. First Brigade was stationed in Baggari County, with Brigadier General Benson Joseph Ufo as its commander. Second Brigade was established in Kpaile County, commanded by Brigadier General John Baptist Uku. Third Brigade was in Bisselia County, and Brigadier General Peter Joseph Ngoli commanded the forces in the area. Finally, Luo forces were small in size, and therefore the Fourth Brigade was established in Jur River, combined with the area of Marial Baii, Kuajiena, and Udici County; the forces were commanded by Brigadier General Majok Thual Thual Madut.

Division 6B, around Raja, was commanded by Major General Musa Ahmed Dakume, and Brigadier General Abdu Yousef Murad was appointed as the deputy commander. Similarly to the forces around Wau, Division 6B was divided into three brigades under the command of Brigadier General Ramadan Future Ramadan Abo, Brigadier General Faisal Fodul Marjan Dor, and Brigadier General Joseph Bangu Waka.

First commander of WBGLFs Sector 7, Lt. Gen. Fayez Fatur (2016)

Prior to the appointment of Major General Salah Momegi Mameri as a governor of Raja State in opposition, on 27 July 2017, both Major General Salah Momegi Mameri and Major General Ashab Khamis Fahl were promoted to the military rank of lieutenant general. Lieutenant General Ashab Khamis Fahl became the deputy sector command, replacing Governor Salah Momegi Mameri.

Discipline amongst the WBGLF

The Western Bahr el Ghazal Lion Forces (WBGLF) generally encompassed Fertit and Luo civilians who were chased by government security forces (predominantly Jieng) during and following the events of 2012 in Wau. They also included retired Fertit and Luo soldiers, as well as professional, well-trained soldiers who defected from government forces, from the army, and from different security forces to join the opposition.

Fertit and Luo civilians arrived in huge numbers, voluntarily joining the WBGLF in order to protect and defend their community.

Lt. Gen. Thomas Bazilio (2016)

Because their aim was to protect their communities (unlike the government forces), the WBGLF never committed human rights violations.

On 14 April 2017, the Western Bahr el Ghazal Lion Forces (WBGLF) allied with the South Sudan People's Liberation Movement and Army in Opposition (SPLM/A-IO). Under the leadership of Dr Riek Machar, they attacked the town of Raja and controlled it for a while after clashing with government troops. During that attack, the entire cabinet of the controversial Lol state fled the city. During their short control of the city, the WBGLF protected the citizens, including Jieng civilians. Unlike the government forces, the opposition forces did not target civilians or their properties.

Also, in order to protect their innocent civilians, who had been slaughtered for two days by the government forces, on 23 June 2016 the WBGLF entered Wau and clashed with the government forces. The WBGLF pulled back with a huge number of Fertit civilians, who were then protected in an area under the opposition forces' control. The

WBGLF shortly captured the city without targeting Jieng civilians or their properties. The WBGLF acted like a professional, modern army.

In 2018, I met a traditional chief of a Jieng tribe, a clan from Aweil area. The chief is a member of the opposition party, SPLM/A-IO. The chief confirmed that he witnessed the attack on Raja. When the WBGLF captured the city, he was inside the city, and afterwards he was able to move around on the street without being intimidated from the opposition forces. The chief explained that the discipline by the opposition was an inspiration to him.

CHAPTER 4

THE ARCSS

South Sudan needed a solution to the crisis that the SPLM/A leadership had created and that caused innocent civilians to suffer. The hope for peace and stability in the Republic of South Sudan was restored when the Agreement on the Resolution of the Conflict in the South Sudan (ARCSS) was signed between the government of South Sudan and the SPLM/A-IO, as represented by President Salva Kiir Mayardit and Chairman and Commander-in-Chief Dr Riek Machar Teny Dhurgon, respectively. The ARCSS was negotiated under mediation of the Intergovernmental Authority for Development (IGAD), which was comprised of Kenya, Uganda, Somalia, Ethiopia, Djibouti, Sudan, and South Sudan

Initially, the government refused to ink the agreement on 17 August 2015 in Addis Ababa, Ethiopia, claiming to have reservations which the mediators had refused to add to the agreement. However, under pressure from the international community (represented by Troika countries, the United Kingdom, the United States of America, Italy, and Norway), the government accepted and signed the agreement in Juba on 26 August 2015 with an attached reservation.

The agreement sought to end the deadly civil war that had broken out in South Sudan in December 2013 following the strained and uneasy political relationship between President Salva Kiir and then Vice President Dr Riek Machar; previously, both were serving in the same government and were within one party, the SPLM/A.

Unfortunately, despite signing the peace agreement with the opposition party, the South Sudanese government refused to admit the presence of

SPLM/A-IO in both the WBG and Equatoria regions. The government further denied the establishment of cantonment areas for the opposition forces in both regions, as stipulated in the ARCSS. The government sometimes claimed that the Western Bahr El Lion Forces were not part of the SPLM/A-IO during the twenty-one months of the civil war. The fact of the matter was that the Jieng developed hatred against Fertit ethnic groups during the Torit Mutiny and the Second Sudanese Civil War, under the leadership of John Garang. During the second civil war, most of the political and military Jieng, including President Salva Kiir, were present.

Many Fertit knew that the Jieng were trying to capture any opportunity, in order to seek revenge for the conflict that had happened during the Qwat Salam in 1985 and 1986.

CHAPTER 5

Rejection of the Newly Created States

Instead of implementing the ARCSS by, for example, appointing the opposition governors in some states as stipulated in the agreement, the president instead violated the agreement, unilaterally increased the number of the states in the country from ten to twenty-eight states, and then upped it to thirty-two states.

In light of the disagreement sparked by the president of the Republic of South Sudan, Salva Kiir Mayardit, insisting on the creation of an illegal thirty-two states in the country, the Southern Sudanese people—and the citizens of the WBG region in particular—loudly rejected the president's decision to create new controversial states in the country. The rejection of the new states was based on several reasons, including the citizens not being consulted. In fact, the members of the Jieng Council of Elders were behind the idea of creating the new states, aiming to expand Jieng territories by annexing others' lands.

In the modern world, the land is regulated and organised for the good of society by a government that citizens trust. But in the Republic of South Sudan, people did not trust the government because leaders in the country had tribal agendas and were corrupt. The South Sudanese people had not yet surrendered their sovereignty to the new state due to this mistrust. With land being both a symbol and the primary source of living for citizens, any regulation, annexation, or grabbing of land by the members of ruling elites, without consultation, would be faced with rejection.

The creation of the new states was controversial and was a violation of the peace agreement signed in August 2015, which had ended the civil war in the young nation. The Resolution of the Conflict in the Republic of South Sudan of August 2015 was signed based on ten states. Therefore, any plan to establish new states in the country required the president consult with his partner in the ARCSS.

Most important, the president was not mandated by the Transitional Constitution of the Republic of South Sudan 2011 (as it was amended) to issue a presidential order concerning increasing the number of states. Therefore, the creation of new states by the president was against the constitution. The constitution further allowed the establishment of new states under conditions of a recommendation initiated by a council of states.

Prior to the presidential decree, there had never been a nationwide consultation regarding increasing the number of states. Neither were there proposals or deliberations at the level of the National Legislative Assembly or the Council of States. Furthermore, there was no involvement of a technical committee in conducting feasibility studies before the presidential order to create new states. Therefore the newly created states were contentious.

The creation of the new states was unpopular amongst the citizens, and the South Sudanese people considered it a surprise move. The president initially rejected the idea of creating more states in the country during the two years of peace negotiations in Addis Ababa with the opposition factions before signing the ARCSS, despite an earlier proposal by the SPLM-IO to create twenty-one federal states for the country. The Intergovernmental Authority on Development (IGAD) then persuaded the SPLM-IO to drop the proposal of creating more states, saying this would be tackled later by all parties in the constitution-making process.

It was not a secret that the creation of the new, controversial states was to the advantage of the Jieng tribe more than other ethnicities in the country. The new map grabbed and annexed other groups' lands to Jiengs. By creating the new thirty-two states, the leaders who stood behind the plan (President Salva Kiir Myaradit and the Jieng Council of Elders) annexed Malakal, Anakdiar, Dolieb Hills, Wau Shilluk, Adar of Mabaan,

Guelguk and Mathiang of Gajaak, Raja of WBG, Pajut of Lou Nuer, Akobo Town of Lou Nuer, both Duk Deng and Kiier in Ayod County, Fangak Pom Zarep, Majiok Nyang, Ulang County of Gajiok Nuer, Kai Kaang and Nyang Malou's territory of Bul Nuer, Kaljaak of Leek Nuer and Manga of Jikany Nuer, and more.

Also, by establishing these controversial states, the president and the Jieng Council of Elders aimed to domestically and internationally blindfold the globe that the Jieng were a majority in South Sudan, scattered all over states. The thirty-two the president created gave his tribe, the Jieng, political advantages, and other minority tribes in the country would be dominated by Jieng.

By creating the new states, the president of the Republic of South Sudan and the Jieng Council of Elders created a condition in which the Jieng dominated both the Upper House and Lower House so they could pursue their tribal interests in Parliament with majority votes.

The map of the new state showed that the president annexed a few oil fields and added them to Jieng lands. This led to other ethnicities in the Southern Sudan completely rejecting the new states. The plan of establishing new states that favoured the Jieng aimed to create a new reality on the ground, whereby Jieng were living in the majority of the oil-producing states.

Annexation of the WBG Land

Unfortunately, the president of the Republic, Salva Kiir Mayardit, had twice violated the Resolution of the Conflict in the Republic of South Sudan (ARCSS) by issuing the presidential decree that increased the number of states from ten to twenty-eight and then to thirty-two states in 2 October 2015 and 14 January 2017, respectively. What was the reason that led the president to violate the agreement? The dividing of the country by the decree significantly shifted the ethnic power balance in South Sudan in the interest of the Jieng. Therefore it became a key point of contestation and was blamed for fuelling the conflict in 2016, particularly in the WBG region.

Like other parts of the country, the creation of the controversial states significantly affected the WBG region, particularly the Raja area.

According to Establishment Order No. 36/2015 AD for the creation of the new South Sudan states, under the new configuration, Western Bahr el Ghazal State was split into two: Wau and the contentious Lol state. Wau maintained its earlier status as the capital of Wau State, which consisted of what used to be Baggari, Bisselia, Kpaile, Kuajiena, Marial Baii, and Udici Counties. Unfortunately, Raja land was annexed to Aweil and was put together with Jieng-dominated Aweil North and Aweil West Counties to make up the new, controversial Lol State. With the inclusion of the two more densely populated Aweil counties, the new boundaries of the controversial Lol State tilted the demographic balance in favour of the Jieng, making the indigenous Fertit ethnic groups a minority in their ancestral lands.

This was not the first time that Raja County had been politically mismanaged. In 1973 it lost its headquarters to Aweil. This latest change was viewed locally as yet another in a series of attempts to expand Jieng dominance in this part of the WBG region.

Lt. Gen. Ashab Khamis Fahl (2019)

Local communities immediately voiced their rejection of Lol State after announcement of the decree on local television. Fertit chiefs in Raja called for a meeting shortly after the decree was announced, and they issued a statement contesting what they viewed as illegal annexation of Raja to Aweil North and Aweil West.

Violation against Fertit under the ARCSS

The security arrangement provision under the ARCSS stipulated that both the government and the SPLM/A-IO forces should be assembled in cantonment areas. Before this provision was agreed to, other opposition forces had already joined the SPLM/A-IO, and the SPLM/A-IO had already mobilised new forces across the country where the conflict had not yet reached. This new recruitment by the opposition party was incentive to the new groups that they would be rewarded with positions in the future national government and army.

In addition, the demilitarising of the capital, stipulated by the ARCSS and putting the capital under United Nation control, had not been implemented. Instead, the government militarised the capital, Juba, and the SPLM/A-IO forces were allowed to travel to Juba to serve as protection guards for the leaders of the SPLM/A-IO. Two rival forces in one place resulted in fighting between the government and the SPLM/A-IO forces.

Throughout the history of the WBG region, Jieng pastoralists have remained a threat to stability in the region. The pastoralists' threats have led to ethnic tension and created several conflicts. One example of this conflict was in 2015, when pastoralist cattle were moved from the Warrap and Lakes areas into Fertit farms in the area around Kpaile, south of Wau. The cattle were accompanied by well-armed cattle keepers from the Jieng tribe. These cattle destroyed crops, and the pastoralists violently attacked the local population. The pastoralists usually used violence to intimidate Fertit farmers, specifically whenever asked to prevent their cattle from destroying the farms. Fertit farmers sent several letters of protest to the governor in Wau, Rizik Zachariah, asking him to interfere and protect the farms. Unfortunately, because the cattle belonged to senior, elite Jieng SPLM/A members who were from Warrap State, the governor ignored the complaints. Eventually, the Fertit began to protect their farms against the pastoralists by chasing away the cattle, which led to rising tension between the two communities. Violence broke out between the farming communities and cattle keepers, with the cattle keepers armed and supported by the government's forces, the SPLA's Fifth Division. As a result, communities from the affected areas fled into the bush, with many seeking support from or joining the Western Bahr el Ghazal Lion Forces.

What had been a conflict between two communities, cattle keepers and farmers, unfortunately led to the first direct clashes between government forces and the WBGLFs in May 2015. From this point, Jieng leaders, particularly President Salva Kiir and the Jieng Council of Elders, began to use public resources to buy heavy modern weapons and recruit more members of Jieng ethnicity in order to implement their plan against Fertit groups, using SPLA forces to drive Fertit ethnic groups from their lands.

Although the government and SPLM/ A-IO had signed the Resolution of the Conflict in the Republic of South Sudan, the ceasefire should have been active in the WBG region between the SPLA and the WBGLF as well. Unfortunately, the government used the clashes between farmers and the cattle keepers as a justification to launch counterinsurgency operations in and around Wau starting in December 2015. The policy of denying the implementation of the peace agreement in the WBG region was from a higher authority, represented by the president and his chief of staff, General Paul Malong Awan.

Then the president and his chief of staff intensified military operations against the WBGLF by sending in the new commander of Fifth Division, Major General Thayip Gatluak Tai. In order to implement their plan, the president and his chief of staff further reinforced the SPLA by sending new Jieng militia and Mathiang Anyor forces. The Mathiang Anyor were predominately Jieng youths from Aweil, Aweil East, Twic, Gogrial, Tonj, Eastern Lakes, Western Lakes, and Gok. The Mathiang Anyor militia were recruited and received their military training under the supervision of Chief of Staff Paul Malong. While transferring to Wau, Mathiang Anyor's only mission was to commit all kinds of ethnic cleansing against the Fertit community.

Since December 2015, as soon as Mathiang Anyor began to implement its mission, tension between the different ethnic groups of Wau town worsened, abuses of Fertit civilians started, and Fertit civilians fled the town. According to Human Rights Watch, these soldiers, mostly from the Jieng tribe, soon began to abuse the local Fertit population, forcing tens of thousands to flee Wau. Many innocent civilians were arrested and then murdered for purportedly being SPLM-IO campaigners.

The attacking and abusing of Fertit civilians by the SPLA and Mathiang

Anyor increased, and the situation deteriorated on 02 October 2015 with President Salva Kiir issuing a presidential decree establishing twenty-eight controversial states in place of the ten constitutionally established states.

From Bad to Worse

The situation remained the same, whereby the government troops and its militia continued their aggression against the Fertit. On 24 December 2015, the president appointed Elias Waya Nyipuoc as governor of Wau State, replacing Rizik Zachariah Hassan, who was been reappointed governor of the controversial Lol State.

After a long period of suppression under Governor Rizik, the appointment of the new governor was seen by the majority of Fertit in the new Wau State as a sign of relief for their long pains under Rizik Zachariah's suppression. Most Wau citizens viewed Elias Waya as somebody who could break the gap and resolve the disagreement between the Jieng and the Fertit, and they hoped he could lower tensions in Wau and bring peaceful coexistence in the city. Therefore on his arrival on 12 January 2016, the people of Wau warmly welcomed the new governor and received him with a huge crowd on the street from Wau's airport to the State Council of Ministers.

During his short term in office, the new governor indeed attempted to bring the situation under control, but without success. The national government continued to extend the Jieng agenda at the expense of Fertit and Luo civilians, leading to the government troops, the SPLA and Mathiang Anyor, violating human rights.

In May 2016, Governor Elias Waya Nyipuoc publicly spoke against the government troops and confirmed that the SPLA and Mathiang Anyor soldiers had killed at least one hundred civilians in a short period. The signing of the ARCSS could have helped the new governor, but there had been no enforcement of the ceasefire signed in August 2015 by the government forces. The aggression against the civilians never stopped, and the government troops continued to attack the Western Bahr el Ghazal Lion Forces around Wau.

In a clear attempt to block the establishment of cantonment sites for

SPLA-IO forces in the WBG region as stipulated in the agreement, the government denied the presence of SPLM/A-IO forces in the WBG region. Instead, the government officials called them bandits in order to justify military operations against them.

However, the SPLA and Mathiang Anyor were repulsed by the WBGLF in most of their attacks. The government troops were faced with heavy resistance from the Western Bahr el Ghazal Lion Forces, and on 8 April 2016 it then deployed Mi-24 helicopters and heavy artillery to attack Wau as clashes continued between the government forces and the WBGLF around the city.

Aggression against the Fertit by both SPLA and Mathiang Anyor forces were characterised by intimidation and killing of Fertit civilians, widespread destruction of properties, looting of food stores, destruction of crops, and displacement of local populations. These arbitrary attacks emerged from villages inhabited mostly by Fertit ethnic groups around Wau. The SPLA and Mathiang Anyor forces substantially increased their presence in Fertit areas of Wau at the beginning of 2016, and residents experienced more harassment and sexual violence. At the same time, the number of Fertit civilians being arbitrary intimidated and detained by security forces increased.

Violation of human Rights

The attacks by government forces on Fertit civilians were serious violations of human rights. These included direct attacks on civilians and indiscriminate attacks against areas in which Fertit civilians were present. Unfortunately, the government forces continuously targeted Fertit civilians whenever they had the chance.

While the Fertit community was under constant attacks by the SPLA and Mathiang Anyor forces, on 18 February 2016 heavily armed Jieng youths attacked Fertit in the west of Wau, following rumours that several Jieng had been killed. While the Jieng youths were attacking local Fertit civilians, soldiers returning from operations outside the town came to their support, setting numerous houses alight in the area of Hai Lokoloko. Jieng soldiers and militia fired indiscriminately on Fertit civilians, killing two men in front of a police station.

As killings and executions continued, the security situation deteriorated the following day, forcing Fertit civilians to abandon their homes and seek refuge in the United Nations Mission in South Sudan's Protection of Civilians site and in churches. This event was followed by an SPLA raid on the hospital that led to the arrests of wounded Fertit patients, on the grounds that any wounded person was likely to be one of the opposition forces. As a result, Fertit patients and staff alike abandoned the hospital.

By March 2016, over sixty thousand civilians from in Wau were displaced. The areas of Hai Nazareth, Hai Ngobu, Hai Kosti, Bazia Jedid, Jebel Rabi, Jebel Khier, Hai Kamsin, and Baggari Jedid were inhabited by Fertit and were particularly targeted and affected by Jieng aggression.

Despite the signing of the peace agreement, the government forces continued attacking the positions of WBGLF forces around Wau and Raja. On 2 April 2016, the South Sudanese government admitted that its forces had attacked locations of opposition forces around Wau, but it said it was fighting against criminals. The opposition forces had confirmed several times that government forces had attacked their cantonment areas in Bussere and Khor-Ghana. The government's offensive was a political move aimed to deny the opposition forces cantonment areas in the WBG region.

Opposition Forces Attack Wau

The government forces, which were predominantly Jieng, continued to implement their plan by carrying out attacks against opposition forces, denying any violation of the peace agreement, and saying repeatedly that their forces were dealing with criminals who were not part of the SPLA-IO.

Denying cantonment areas in the WBG region was state policy. All Jieng officials were involved, accusing the WBGLF of being criminals and not an ally with the main opposition forces, the SPLM/A-IO. On 7 April 2016, the head of Information and Public Relations in the South Sudanese army, Brigadier General Malaak Ayuen, said on a television channel owned by the state that the SPLM-IO had no forces in the Western Bahr al-Ghazal region. "Those in Western Bahr el-Ghazal are not part of IO; they are not covered by the agreement and it is the right of government forces to deal with such elements."

The government troops continued putting the lives of innocent civilians under threat. In order to protect Fertit civilians inside Wau, on 23 June 2016, the WBGLF entered Wau, and a heavy battle broke out between SPLA and WBGLF south of the state capital. After occupying the town, the WBGLF pulled back, with a large number of civilians, to their positions outside of Wau. Those civilians sought refuge in areas under the control of the WBGLF, an opposition group allied to the SPLM/A-IO and led by Dr Riek Machar. As result, a state of emergency was declared in Wau, and the soldiers of the SPLA's Fifth Division moved into town, arresting, torturing, and killing unarmed Fertit civilians. These forces that committed human right violations were under the command of Lieutenant General Gabriel Jok Riak, who had been accused of human rights abuses by the United Nations. On 2 May 2018, General Gabrial Jok was appointed the president's new chief of staff, replacing Lieutenant General James Ajongo.

Commander of Division 6A, Maj. Gen. Abdullah Ujang (2019)

During his term in office, the new governor tried to encourage the government army to respect and implement the ARCSS in order to protect civilians. Unfortunately, his attempts ran counter to the intentions of the higher authority, represented by the president and his chief of staff, who wanted to suppress the Fertit. Governor Waya was seen by Jieng elites as somebody who sympathised with Fertit civilians. Therefore on 24 June 2016, President Kiir sacked Governor Waya and arrested him.

SPLA Attacking Fertit Civilians

As a result of Elias Waya's dismissal, on the evening of 24 June 2016, heavily armed Jieng youths shot randomly in areas known to be predominantly Fertit. The attackers were Jieng militia in civilian clothes supported by the government forces, and they moved from house to house attacking civilians with machetes, firearms, sticks, and spears, as well as engaging in widespread looting. Violence continued throughout the night and resulted in many Fertit civilian deaths.

The fighting displaced more than seventy thousand Fertit civilians within Wau, including at the Catholic church, the South Sudan Red Cross compound, St Joseph's, Nazareth, Lokoloko and the UNMISS PoC site. Twelve thousand Fertit civilians sought shelter near the UNMISS base alone. Additionally, more than fifty thousand Fertit civilians (including my mother) fled to Ngo Halima, Tadu, and Ngisa, areas under control of opposition forces.

This time the attack by Jieng forces was severe and constituted crimes against humanity and ethnic cleansing. The Fertit civilians who sought shelter in the compound of the Catholic cathedral in Wau described the terrible aggressions by the government forces against them. They recalled how government soldiers and armed Jieng youths attacked neighbourhoods inhabited by ethnic Fartit. A two-year-old boy was shot in the arms. A woman was violently raped in the street. Fertit who stayed in their homes in order to protect their properties from looting were killed in their houses.

A Fertit civilian stated that he was at home when the shooting started. He saw soldiers from the SPLA shooting at civilians. This civilian said that he grabbed his children and ran for safety towards the cathedral. On his way, he saw government soldiers gun down three members of his family.

Attacks against civilians, rather than direct confrontations with the WBGLF, was a feature of government soldiers during the civil war. The Amnesty International confirmed in their report in August 2017 that government forces and Jieng militia carried out indiscriminate attacks on civilian towns and villages, killed civilians, systematically looted civilian properties, and forcibly displaced tens of thousands of civilians from their land.

Meanwhile, inside Wau tensions continued with multiple violent incidents on a daily basis. Security forces together with the Jieng youth continued their violence against Fertit civilians. This led to the WBGLF fighting back by attacking perceived perpetrators in self-defence. This reaction by Fertit forces further increased the cycle of revenge killings as security inside Wau and the surrounding area deteriorated even more.

The worst cycle of revenge attacks by Jieng against Fertit civilians occurred when SPLA officers went on patrol into Kpaile area. The officers had gone outside the town to deliver military supplies and command operations against the Western Bahr el Ghazal Lion Forces.

Unfortunately, on their return to Wau, the SPLA convoy was ambushed by the WBGLF on 9 April 2017. The incident led to the deaths of several senior government soldiers, including the head of military operations in Wau, Brigadier Peter Par, and Abraham Bol Chut Dhuol, who was the head of military logistics and the younger brother of the Western Lakes Governor, Major General Matur Chut Dhuol.

Immediately after the ambush, on 10 April 2017 the members of Jieng Council of Elders had an urgent meeting in Juba in order to deliberate on the death of the two officers. In the meeting, they decided to take revenge by instigating more attacks, looting and burning houses related to the Fertit ethnic groups in Wau. As a result, instead of attacking the WBGLF, on 10 April 2017 the government forces inside Wau carried out what was planned by the members of the JCE: revenge killings and what was considered to be the collective punishment of Fertit, leading to the deaths of many civilians, including Michael Mboro, who was killed in the Nazareth area. The government troops targeted Fertit civilians, which resulted in the burning of houses in neighbourhoods perceived to be Fertit, a well as the arrest of youths and some humanitarian aid workers.

PART 4

CHAPTER 1

RENEWAL OF THE CONFLICT

The signing of Resolution of the Conflict in the Republic of South Sudan (ARCSS) resulted in the formation of a Transitional Government of National Unity (TGoNU) on 29 April 2016. Dr Riek Machar, who had fled Juba following the outbreak of the civil war in 2013, served as vice president.

Unfortunately, because the Jieng elites lacked the political will and were afraid of any reform in the country, the government began to misinterpret and resist the implementation of the agreement. Thereafter, the regime in Juba intimidated and targeted members of the opposition party inside Juba, starting with the incident on 3 July 2016 in which government security shot at a soldier of SPLM/A-IO, Lieutenant Colonel George Gismallah.

The government continued its aggression against members of opposition party with another event on 7 July 2016. The opposition force, loyal to Dr Riek Machar, was attacked by government troops at a checkpoint inside Juba. The incident left five members of the government forces dead and two injured from opposition forces. In the second day of the event, on the night of 8 July 2016 inside the presidential palace J1, there were violent confrontations between the government and SPLM/A-IO. The violence spread into many parts of the city, resulting in the deaths of many soldiers and civilians as well, along with the destruction of property and the displacement of people.

This incident was a deliberate attempt to assassinate Vice President Dr Riek Machar. It was orchestrated by the president of the Republic,

Salva Kiir Mayardit, when he invited his vice president to have a meeting in the presidential palace, J1. An exchange of fire between the two forces occurred and resulted in intensive shooting in which the clashes between forces loyal to President Salva Kiir and those loyal to Vice President Riek Machar. About thirty-five of the SPLA-IO soldiers who had been deployed on the street outside J1 were killed instantly, and over eighty died from the government forces.

Concerning the WBG region, particularly Wau, the violence never stopped after the signing of the ARCSS. The government forces continued their military operations against the opposition army in the WBG region, represented by the WBGLF. The government, under the leadership of President Salva Kiir, refused to treat the WBGLF as part of the SPLA-IO. Instead, the government called the WBGLF bandits in order to justify its military operations against them.

Therefore in order to quietly target the WBGLF, who were in full control of areas around Wau and Raja, the government deployed National Security Service forces in late April 2017 to monitor the civilians inside the town after the violence that took place in Wau, where Jieng soldiers and allied Jieng youth were targeting ethnic Fertit and Luo civilians.

The NSS activated patrols with the police to improve the security situation inside the city—and in order to lure displaced Fertit civilians to return to their houses. The displaced people were afraid of a renewal of aggression and refused to return, with some of them cautiously able to visit their houses only during day time. However, significant parts of Wau, especially Fertit areas, were heavily affected by the fighting and remained abandoned and desolate.

Fertit civilians in Wau, including those living within the United Nations Mission in South Sudan's Protection of Civilians site, described the abuses they were subjected to as ethnic cleansing and crimes against them, preventing them from returning to their homes.

Government Restriction on Aid Agencies

The damages that the government of South Sudan, under the leadership of President Salva Kiir Mayardit, caused to citizens turned one of the richer countries in the area, with huge natural resources, into a poor country. Now the citizens had to depend on humanitarian assistance.

Unfortunately, the only alternative to survive, which the majority of the South Sudanese people were rely on, was being prevented by the government. The government began to use food as a weapon against its own civilians. The regime in Juba had been implementing a policy that led to many internally displaced persons (IDPs), mostly Fertit civilians, suffering and starving inside and around Wau, specifically in Baggari, Bisselia, Kpaile, Wadhalelo, and Bururud.

The regime in Juba had been using several mechanisms to block the distribution of food by nongovernmental organisations (NGOs) in order to create hunger amongst IDPs in and around Wau.

- At the beginning of 2017, the state authority ordered the NGOs to reduce the food supply arriving into Wau.
- From April 2017, the regime in Juba began to forbid NGOs from distributing food items to the IDPs, predominantly Fertit and Luo tribes, in the area under control of the WBGLF around Wau, specifically in Baggari, Bisselia, Kpaile, and some parts of Kuajiena. In this regard, the UNMISS issued a statement in which it expressed its concern. "Government preventing aid from the needy people to relieve them of their suffering is a clear human rights violation by the regime in Juba."
- The IDPs inside the UNMISS PoC and Wau churches raised the concern about the shortage of food items on 9 June 2017. Those IDPs survived without food distribution from the NGOs for two months, as a result of the authority in Juba pressuring and discouraging NGOs from supplying food in Wau.
- For four consecutive months until July 2017, the government's National Security Services in Wau directly ordered the NGOs to halt their distribution of food items to the IDPs inside Wau Church, Loku Loku Church, Nazareth Church, and Saint Joseph Church, with the aim of starving the IDPs and forcing them to return to their houses.
- The regime in Juba deployed a battalion of government troops with heavy artillery each to Baggari, Bisselia, Kpaile, and around

Kuajiena (in Wadhalelo, Agur, Akow, Dang Acha, Umbilli, and Channa). They killed civilians, destabilised farmers and destroyed their agriculture crops, looted properties, and burned civilian houses.

- In June 2018, the UNMISS expressed its concerns over the situation of Fertit civilians affected by the conflict in the Baggari, Bisselia, and Kpaile areas. The report by the UNMISS stated that the situation was deteriorating as a result of aid workers and the Ceasefire Monitoring Commission being prevented from reaching these areas by the government forces. The mission also revealed that the World Food Program (WFP) survey team had been harassed and threatened several times, especially in the Ngo Baggari area, by the SPLA.

3. In August 2018, the local authority besieged the UNMISS PoC site in Wau, preventing distribution of food to the IDPs inside the UNMISS camp. The government accused them of being rebels and threatened to storm the camp and attack civilians.

Commander of Division 6B, Maj. Gen. Musa Dakumi (2019)

Government troops chased a large number of Fertit civilians away from the cities. For example, the civilians who took refuge in cities away from government troops, such as Forjomoi and Gide in Kpaile, remained without basic services. The prevention of NGOs from entering the liberated areas (the areas under control of the opposition army) led to a large number of civilians, especially children, living without schools. Those civilians were still hiding in these cities after the signing of R-ARCSS because they did not trust the government troops.

The Jieng elites, who were politicians and military men, utilised public resources to buy weapons and recruit their youth against the South Sudanese opposition, instead of using the money to build the country. Some Jieng officials made public their intention to resolve the conflict militarily, leaving the country without development for a long time.

The humanitarian situation in the country continued to worsen. As of February 2019, an estimated six million, or half of the population of the country, were at risk of hunger. That was added to already two million South Sudanese civilians who were facing extreme starvation.

In early 2019, the Norwegian Refugee Council (NRC) was quoted as saying, "Despite the peace agreement signed five months ago, conflict continues to impact the lives of hundreds of thousands of people. Not just by the daily torment of fearing guns and violence, but by the daily torment of feeling hungry and watching your child suffer from starvation." And yet the government still pushed for the renewal of conflict.

CHAPTER 2

THE SIGNING OF ACOH

The security situation in the Western Bahr el Ghazal region remain poor, with a large number of the Fertit population taking refuge in the UNMISS PoC for safety. However, on 21 December 2017 the parties to the conflict signed the Agreement on Cessation of Hostilities, Protection of Civilians, and Humanitarian Access (ACOH) in Addis Ababa. The agreement to cessation of hostilities was reached after the government of South Sudan, opposition parties, and other key stakeholders agreed to revitalise the 2015 peace agreement brokered by the Intergovernmental Authority on Development (IGAD).

Under the terms of the ACOH draft, which the two sides immediately accepted, the forces from both sides were supposed to stop engaging in physical and media fighting. The agreement was meant to pave the way for further negotiations, based on the ARCSS, to resolve the crisis in the country.

The agreement was built on several positive steps to be immediately implemented by the parties in order to stabilise the country, bring the warring parties to the negotiation table, and protect civilians. First, the ACHO called for an immediate cessation of hostilities. Second, the agreement called on the two parties to stop media campaigns and propaganda statements against each other. Third, it called for allowing humanitarian access to assist internally displaced persons, especially in the UNMISS PoC, churches, and the areas under the control of opposition forces. Fourth, it called for the withdrawal of foreign troops from South

Sudan's territories. The ACOH further included other articles, such as a full release of all political detainees and prisoners of war in the country.

As with the previous agreement in 2015, the opposition parties were fully committed to the agreement. But unfortunately, the government had hidden agendas. Therefore the government did not fully implement the ACHO, particularly in the WBG region. The government considered the Fertit opposition as antagonistic and not part of the agreement. The regime in Juba instead used the ACHO to proceed with their revenge killing against the Fertit ethnic groups.

Violation of ACOH

The government troops had halted military operations across other parts of the country, but the aggressions continued in Equatoria and the WBG region. The targeting of both the Fertit civilians and the WBGLF (predominantly Fertit Luo) by the government troops (predominantly members Jieng) continued despite the signing of Agreement of Cessation of Hostilities, Protection of Civilians and Humanitarian Access (ACOH). While the opposition parties, including the WBGLF, fully implemented the ACOH by releasing all prisoners of war and halting their military operations except in self-defence, the government troops were still on the offensive.

The aggressions by the government troops against the Fertit and Luo never stopped. Access for the nonprofit organisations to deliver the humanitarian aid was denied. Some political detainees and prisoners of war in other parts of the country had been released, but in the WBG region things remained unclear. Since 2012, the prisoners had remained in detention in Wau's prison.

Brig. Gen. Majok Thual Thual (2018)

The attacks on WBGLF positions had been well planned in the past by Jieng elites in the national government and then implemented by local authorities. For example, just a week before the signing of ACOH, on 13 December 2017 during his visit to Wau State, Tambura State Governor Patrick Raphael Zomoi discussed with his counterpart, Angelo Taban Biajo, a possible attack on opposition forces in the area, represented by the WBGLF. Their aim of attacking of the position of the opposition forces was to forcefully reopen the road between the two states. Also, on 15 June 2018, Governor Angelo Taban Biajo invited the newly appointed commander of the SPLA's Fifth Division in Wau State, Major General Thayip Gatluak, to his house, where they made a plan to attack the positions of the opposition forces around Wau City. During their plan, since 2 July 2018, the number of government troops was reinforced, followed by serious attempts to capture the opposition forces' strongholds, particularly around Baggari, Bisselia, Kpaile, and Kuajiena. In their attempts to capture the positions of the opposition forces around Wau City, the government forces faced heavy resistance by the WBGLF. The opposition forces in the WBG region, and particularly around Wau State, were under the command of Lieutenant General Ashab Khamis Fahl, Major General Abdullah Ujang, Brigadier Majok Thual Madut, and Brigadier General Peter Joseph. They had been inflicting heavy casualties on the government troops and captured several military reinforcements, including vehicles, during that period. However, the WBGLF lost some strategic positions, particularly in Bisselia, Baggari, and Wadhalelo.

Below are few of the government violations.

- As a result of the government forces violating the agreement by attacking the position of opposition forces around Raja, six thousand civilians arrived in South Kordufan, the Sudanese town bordering South Sudan. This was followed by more refugees from the area in 2017.
- Wadhalelo had been under control of the opposition forces since early 2017. However, with arrival of General Thayip Gatluak, on 11 June 2018 the government troops attacked and captured the position of WBGLF in Wadhalelo, where they targeted Luo civilians and their houses. The Luo civilians were displaced into the bushes.
- With a clear violation of the agreement signed between the two warring parties, on 23 June 2018 the government troops made multiple attacks on the Baggari and Mboro areas, though the WBGLF repulsed these attacks. However, the SPLA attacked the area again and then took control of the Mboro area on the second day after heavy resistance; they occupied the main clinic and one school as their base.
- On 26 June 2018, the WBGLF repulsed multiple attacks by government troops in Ngo Baggari and Ngissa.
- On the second day, on 27 June 2018, the WBGLF again repulsed an attack on the Ngo Khaki area. However, extensive attacks by the government troops led innocent Fertit civilians to be destabilised in some areas, often multiple times. As a result, the places they fled to also came under attack by the SPLA. For instance, when the Fertit civilians came under attack in Mboro, they fled to Ngo Pere, but the government forces followed them and aggressively attacked the civilians again.
- On 6 July 2018, another violation by the government on the Ngo Khaki region resulted in opposition forces and civilians being

pulled from the area, leaving the government troops to destroy and loot the civilian properties. The looted civilians' properties, especially the school properties, were relocated by the government forces to their areas.

- However, after the government troops had been chased out by the opposition forces, on 9 July 2018 government troops attacked Mboro again, where they killed three civilians and arrested three civilians, including Lewis Maborok.
- On 22 July 2018, the WBGLF repulsed an attack on their position in Ngo Dagalla, and they captured a large number of military supplies.
- On 10 August 2018, the WBGLF surrounded the government forces in Natabu. The government forces were on their way to reinforce their follow SPLA, who were attacking and looting civilian properties in Ngo Baggari.
- The repeated attacks by the government troops on the positions of the WBGLF, which was under the umbrella of the SPLM/A-IO, led to Taban, Ngo Baggari, Wadhalelo, Mboro, and other areas being captured by government troops.

As the result of the government violating the ACOH, by 16 September 2018, just before the signing of R-ARCSS, the government forces had captured more territories from the opposition forces and pushed deep into the areas around Mboro, Baggari and Wadhalelo, as well as the Taban area in Kpaile. They violently displaced Fertit and Luo civilians, destroyed civilian infrastructures such as farms and markets, and occupied humanitarian infrastructures such as clinics and schools. This worsened the humanitarian situation because the NGOs were denied access to these areas.

The SPLM/A Admit Destruction of the Country

On 4 May 2018, the senior members of National Liberation Council (NLC) of the ruling party, the SPLM, met in Juba and concluded their meeting with a final resolution admitting to the public that they'd failed to meet the expectations of the people of the country. They issued a statement admitting to the following.

1. Failing to respect the SPLM/A's institution and bring democracy in their party, which was described mostly by South Sudanese people as the root cause of the crisis in the Republic of South Sudan since independence.
2. Their collective responsibility, as leaders of the ruling party SPLM, for the crises that had brought destruction to the country, particularly the party's power struggle that started in 2013 and resulted in a civil war. The SPLM party became the direct cause for the suffering of the South Sudanese people.
3. Their loss of discipline and respect of basic rules of the SPLM party. The lack of discipline amongst the members negatively contributed to the emergence of the 2013 and 2016 crises over power and leadership.

On the peace dissemination tour to Bahr el Ghazal, President Salva Kiir Mayardit witnessed the damages caused by his ruling party, the SPLM, and the SPLA. In a public rally in Wau Stadium on 5 March 2019, as the leader of the ruling party, President Salva Kiir Mayardit asked the South Sudanese people for forgiveness for his party's responsibility for the damages in the past. He admitted that his party, the SPLM/A, was the cause of the suffering.

Sadly, in this public rally, the president refrained from apologising to the people of the WBG for the killing and destruction caused by his troops since the shooting of peaceful protestors in 2012. Also, he failed to answer the people of the WBG region demanding their rights. The annexation of their land remained, although the president asked for reconciliation.

Indeed, most of the observers cited that the innocent South Sudanese citizens didn't commit any wrongdoing that warranted being killed or destabilised by the ruling party, the SPLM/A. The proximate cause of this brutal civil war was a power struggle amongst the top leadership of SPLM, as the president admitted publicly after five years of ignorance.

At the same Wau rally, the president offered his apology for the events from 2013 to 2016 which caused the suffering of the civilians around the country. Unfortunately, the president did not mention the tragic event of 2012 in Wau City, where the government forces shot at and killed several peaceful protestors.

Given the fact that the members of the NLC and of the ruling party, under the leadership of President Salva Kiir Mayardit, admitted to the public and took full responsibility for their irresponsibility, this confirmed the allegations by many that the party, under their current leadership, had no vision to rule the country democratically, develop its economy, and create a country that the people of the South Sudan dreamed and voted for in the referendum of 2011.

Although the government admitted to being both the causes and the tools of perpetrating mass destruction, rape, and killing against innocent civilians, the regime in Juba still committed more atrocities. History will hold the leadership of the SPLM/A accountable for their actions.

- Killing, raping, and committing abuses against innocent civilians in different places throughout the Republic of South Sudan.
- Evil acts of destruction and pillaging civilian property during government operations in several areas in the Republic of South Sudan.
- Destabilising innocent civilians as the result. Until January 2019, the UNMISS continued to shelter 1,854,000 internally displaced person around the country; these IDPs were forced to flee their homes due to irresponsible behaviour by the SPLM/A party.
- Furthermore, as the SPLM/A continuously waged war on its own people, many civilians fled the country, bringing the total number of refugees in 2018, according the UNHCR, to 2,274,387, scattered in the countries bordering the South Sudan. Those refugees sheltered in the Sudan totalled 852,080, and Uganda (768,099), Ethiopia (422,240), Kenya (115,240), and the Democratic Republic of Congo (95,704) also contained South Sudanese refugees.
- In addition to the wide range of mismanagement of public resources by SPLM leaders, looting the resources of the country continued on a daily basis, leaving civilians without basic needs.

Large financial transactions involving politically exposed persons, defined as SPLM senior government officials and military officers as well as their families, ended up in personal accounts outside the country.

As the SPLM/A and its history of liberation was considered a great movement that played a significant role in the liberation of the country, the people of South Sudan quickly became sceptical about the future of the country under the leadership of the SPLM party.

CHAPTER 3

THE SIGNING OF R-ARCSS

Although the government forces were continuously on the offensive in the WBG and Equatoria regions, the SPLM/A-IO, under the leadership of Dr Riek Machar, continued to engage with the government in order to find a lasting solution to the conflict in the Republic of South Sudan (RSS). As a result of negotiation mediated by the Intergovernmental Authority on Development (IGAD), on 12 September 2018 the government of South Sudan and the opposition parties—including the SPLM/A-IO, Other Political Parties (OPP), South Sudanese Opposition Alliance (SSOA), the SPLM Former Detainees (FDs), Umbrella of Political Parties, National Alliance of Political Parties, United Sudan African Party (USAF), African National Congress (ANC), and others—signed the Revitalised Agreement on the Resolution of the Conflict in South Sudan (R-ARCSS).

Unfortunately, the mediators of the R-ARCSS designed the agreement to give incentives for political and military elites in order to accept the peace. It employed a large number of civil and military men from both sides on the government payroll.

Also, the peace agreement created huge risk for its implementation. For example, the agreement encouraged the government to recruit a new private militia in order to prepare for another war. A previous agreement, the ARCSS, experience showed that the provision that stipulated the military unification and the Disarmament, Demobilisation, and Reintegration (DDR) resulted in new recruitment and increases in the number of government forces for military preparedness, political guarantees, and corruption. Therefore, similar to the ARCSS, the R-ARCSS seemed to be a method for both the government and the opposition parties to prepare for a new round of conflict or corruption.

However, unlike the ARCSS of 2015, the international community, represented by China, Japan, Russia, the European Union, the Troika of the United States of America, the United Kingdom, Italy, and Norway, was cautious and suspicious about the political will of the parties to implement the new agreement. The international community even refrained from cosigning the agreement. The reason behind their caution was specifically related to the government continuing to dishonour past agreements. The regime in Juba never honoured its obligations to previous agreements such as the ARCSS and the ACOH.

Since the civil war had renewed on 8 July 2016, the security situation in Wau and the surrounding area remained largely under aggression by government troops. Despite the signing of ACOH, the government continued to attack opposition positions around Wau and Raja and recaptured some previously held territories. These offensives were undertaken in violation of multiple ceasefire agreements that had been signed, including a permanent one that was inked on 27 June 2018 and then violated within hours.

Unfortunately, the signing of R-ARCSS did not stop the government from attacking the WBGLF and Fertit civilians. According to the R-ARCSS, the government and the opposition parties would have a Pre-Transitional Period of eight months, followed by forming a Revitalised Transitional Government of National Unity (RTGoNU). The RTGoNU would function for thirty-six months, followed by a general election in the country.

In a step seen by the majority of the South Sudanese people, due to rewording by those who caused the crisis, the power sharing was divided amongst the same party who had caused the conflict, with Salva Kiir remaining president of the Republic of South Sudan and Dr Riek Machar being reinstated as the first vice president.

For the first time in the history of the country, in addition to the first vice president, there would be four vice presidents in the Republic of South Sudan. The move would divert most of the oil revenue from development to financing the politicians.

Director of NSS Brig. Gen. Sharif Dee (2018)

The R-ARCSS was a very typical payroll political agreement. The agreement provided huge public posts for the two parties. In the executive position, the R-ARCSS called for the creation of the RTGoNU, which would include a Council of Ministers which shall comprise thirty-five ministries. The ministerial position should be distributed amongst the parties as follows: twenty ministries for the incumbent TGoNU, under President Salva Kiir; nine ministries for SPLM/A-IO; three ministries for the South Sudan Opposition Alliance (SSOA); two ministries for Former Detainees (FDs); and one ministry for Other Political Parties (OPP).

In addition to the Council of Ministers, the R-ARCSS provided restructure of the Transitional National Legislative Assembly (TNLA) and the Council of States by adding more from opposition parties. The new TNLA was composed of 550 members to be shared amongst the parties as follow: the TGoNU with 332 members, the SPLM/A-IO with 128 members, the SSOA with 50 members, the OPP with 30 members, and the FDs with 10 members. The increase of TNLA members by the agreement would negatively affect the budget. The government would need to build new, larger premises in order to accommodate the new Members of Parliament.

The agreement also divided the public posts on the state level amongst the parties: the incumbent TGoNU at 55 per cent, the SPLM/A-IO at 27 per cent, the SSOA at 10 per cent, and the OPP at 8 percent.

On the controversial number of the states' issues, according to the R-ARCSS, within two weeks of the signing of the agreement, the IGAD Executive Secretariat would appoint an Independent Boundaries Commission (IBC) for the Republic of South Sudan. The IBC's tasks was to consider recommendations on the number of states in the Republic of South Sudan, their boundaries, and the composition and restructuring of the Council of States, all within a maximum of ninety days that shall not be extendable.

In the event that the IBC failed to make its final recommendation on the number of the states before the end of its term, the IBC would automatically be transformed into the Referendum Commission on Number and Boundaries of States (RCNBS), and it would organise a referendum.

Regarding the number of the states, the agreement provided that IGAD mediation would appoint a Technical Boundary Committee (TBC) which would define and demarcate the tribal areas of South Sudan as they stood on 1 January 1956 and the tribal areas in dispute in the country.

In order for the warring parties to forgive and reconcile, according to the R-ARCSS, prisoners of war and political detainees would be released immediately and handed over to the International Committee of the Red Cross and Crescent (ICRC).

In the R-ACSSS, the parties declared their commitment to a federal and democratic system of governance being enacted during the permanent constitution-making process.

On the establishment of a new constitution in the country, within six months of its signing, the R-ARCSS call for a reconstituted National Constitutional Amendment Committee (NCAC). The NCAC was tasked with incorporating the agreement into the Transitional Constitution of the Republic of South Sudan reviewing the Political Parties Act of 2012, and ensuring that the act complied with international best practices for the free and democratic registration of political parties in South Sudan.

Lack of the accountability since the independence of the country remained one of the causes of the conflict. Therefore, the R-ARCSS also provided that upon establishment, the RTGoNU would initiate legislation for the establishment of the Commission for Truth, Reconciliation, and Healing (CTRH); the Hybrid Court for South Sudan (HCSS); and the Compensation and Reparation Authority (CRA).

On paper, the R-ARCSS seemed to be the only alternative to addressing all root causes of the conflict in the Republic of the South Sudan and reforming the country to be a democratic country. However, lack of political will and uncertainty about the future of government contribution remained challenging, especially during the pretransitional period.

The Jieng elites continued to put up obstacles in order to prevent the implementation of the R-ARCSS. Based on the R-ARCSS, there should be several committees to establish during the pretransitional period of eight months. The remaining committees were to be formed after the pretransitional period or after the formation of the RTGoNU. The following committees and mechanisms were to be formed and reconstituted during the beginning of the pretransitional period.

- National Pre-Transitional Committee (NPTC)
- National Constitutional Amendment Committee (NCAC)
- Reconstituted Ceasefire and Transitional Security Arrangements Monitoring and Verification Mechanism (R-CTSAMVM)
- Reconstituted Joint Monitoring and Evaluation Commission (R-JMEC)
- Independent Boundaries Commission (IBC)
- Technical Boundary Committee (TBC)
- Joint Defence Board (JDB)
- Joint Military Ceasefire Commission (JMCC)
- Joint Transitional Security Committee (JTSC)
- Strategic Defence and Security Review Board (SDSRB)
- Area Joint Military Ceasefire Commissions (AJMCC)
- Joint Military Ceasefire Teams (JMCT)

Under pressure of the international community and the people of South Sudan, during the first stages of the pretransitional period, some of the committees, such as CTSAMM, JMEC, NPTC, and NCAC, were formed. Some were renamed in accordance to the timeframe of the implementation matrix. However, other committees—such as JDB,

JMCC, JTSC, SDSRB, AJMCC, JMCT, and TBC—were tactically delayed by the government to be formed later than the specified timeline in the implementation matrix. Other committees have not been established as of February 2019.

CHAPTER 4

VIOLATION OF R-ARCSS

Both the ARCSS and the R-ARCSS were repeatedly structured as incentives to mobilise for new recruits, which helped lay the seeds for the next round of conflict. Disputes amongst the signatories arose because these agreement did not fully and immediately address the root causes of the conflict. Also, the reason for disputes may have been related to unfair allocation of both civil and military positions. Therefore from day one, many South Sudanese and observers were sceptical about the agreement and questioned whether the R-ARCSS would create stability and bring urgently needed reforms in the country.

This caution appears to be shared by the Troika countries, the United States of America, the United Kingdom, Italy, and Norway, who declined to cosign the agreement. They had seen that the government dishonoured the ARCSS of 2015 and continued to commit violations of the previous ceasefire agreements since the conflict started in December 2013. The international community and the South Sudanese people would like to see evidence of the parties' commitment to accountable implementation of the R-ARCSS.

There were plenty of reasons for the people of the country be sceptical about the R-ARCSS. Months after signing the agreement, the government remained on offensive, attacking opposition forces in several areas, particularly in the WBG and Equatorian regions. Access to humanitarian aid was hindered, and the workers were detained and attacked by the government troops. Lack of media freedom still existed, and sexual abuses and violations of human rights increased.

In the Western Bahr el Ghazal region, despite the signing of the R-ARCSS in 2018, the situation was similar to the ARCSS of 2015. The government continued to dishonour the agreement, and attacks on the Fertit never halted. The WBGLF, an ally of the SPLM/A-IO around Wau, was pushed out of its previously controlled areas in Baggari, Bisselia, and Wadhalelo, particularly in the period around October 2018, but it still controlled areas to the south and far south-west of Wau, as well as most of the area around Raja.

The government, under the leadership of President Salva Kiir Mayardit, continued to violate the agreement (specifically in the WBG region) because Jieng political and military leaders felt hatred against Fertit ethnic groups. Therefore their attempts to dominate the WBG region would likely continue by all means, with or without the peace agreement. Despite efforts by all parties to resolve the conflict in the Republic of South Sudan, the Jieng elites had no interest in bringing stability and development to the country.

Fertit and Luo volunteers, WBGLF (2017).

As of October 2018, the towns and villages in Agur, Akau, Ngo Dakalla, Farajallah Ngissa, Gedi, Gitan, Tirga, Bo Bridge, and a few others remained under control of the opposition forces, the WBGLF. As a result of the government forces violating the ceasefire agreement with more aggression, the areas which had been previously occupied by the opposition forces (Mboro, Biringi, Ngo Baggari, Taban, Ngoku, and Wadhalelo) were captured by government forces.

Despite the signing of the R-ARCSS, government troops continued to attack the positions of the WBGLF. Below are some of the violations committed by the government troops and the counterattacks by the opposition forces.

- The government officials, predominately Jieng elites, continued to keep prisoners of war in the WBG region, especially in Wau. In August 2018, the Human Rights Watch raised its concern about the government's unwillingness to release the political detainees and POWs as stipulated in the both the ACOH and the R-ARCS. The rights groups said hundreds more continued to be held without trial and were not allowed visits from their families and lawyers.
- On 24 September 2018, government troops launched attacks on opposition-controlled areas in Ngo Baggari and Faragallah.
- The WBGLF recaptured their previously held positions by attacking government forces in Wadhalelo between 25 and 29 September 2018, and in Mboro on 26 September 2018.
- After the government forces, in violation of agreement, captured several areas which were previously controlled by opposition forces, the WBGLF launched a counterattack on the government's position in Bissellia and Baggari on 25 September 2018. The WBGLF recaptured the positions they'd previously held.
- On 26 September 2018, the government forces went to Ngo Baggari, attacked the position of the opposition forces, burnt houses, destroyed agriculture crops, and looted civilian properties (including school properties). The looted school properties had been moved by government forces to the areas where the Jieng inhabited.

- On 26 September 2018, the government troops attacked the opposition's position in the Ngo Kazi area, during which SPLA allegedly killed one civilian, abducted three people, and looted civilian properties.

- On 2 October 2018, the WBGLF attacked the government forces' positions in the Natabu area and recaptured the area. On the same day, the president officially changed the name of SPLA to the South Sudan People's Defence Forces (SSPDF).

- On 3 October 2018, the government forces renewed coordinated attacks against the opposition troops in Farajalla, Ngo Baggari, Ngo Kbere, and Mboro. On the same day, the SSPDF launched another attack in Ngo Ku that continued through 13 October 2018. In these battles, the government forces used internationally banned weapons to push back opposition forces. After the WBGLF was pushed back, the government troops then targeted civilians, burnt houses, destroyed crops, and looted properties in the area.

- As the government forces were faced with heavy resistance from opposition troops, the regime in Juba brought more military reinforcements into Wau State. Further, with more violations of the agreement, the government began to train new recruits at the Mapel military training base in order for local state authorities to increase their manpower and invade Fertit areas. As a result, on 9 October 2018 a huge SSPDF force moved towards Kpaile County and was stationed in the Bussere, Taban, and Dokorongo areas. Despite heavy resistance, the Jieng elites were determined to proceed with their tribal plan of chasing away the Fertit from their lands.

- The attacks by government forces intensified, although there were heavy casualties. On 11 October 2018, the SSPDF attacked the positions of WBGLF, an ally to SPLM/A IO, in Ngo Ku. The SSPDF controlled the area, terrorised many civilians, killed innocent citizens, and looted and destroyed property. The properties looted by government forces were relocated by the SPLA forces to the neighbouring (Jieng) states. The government forces further made several arrests in Ngo Ku, including three women.

- On 12 October 2018, in the early morning a large number of government forces attacked civilians in Ngissa, Ngo Ku, and Dadou. They killed fifty-six civilians and destroyed properties and farms. The government troops committed ethnic cleansing against the Fertit civilians, who sought refuge in the areas under WBGLF control. In this location, as in other areas, there were no opposition forces.

- On 25 October 2018, the government forces prevented a convoy of humanitarian aid from entering into the liberated areas controlled by the WBGLF. The convoy included the United Nation Mission in South Sudan (UNMISS), the Ceasefire and Transitional Security Arrangement Monitoring Mechanism (CTSAMMVM), and the Community Empowerment for Progress Organisation (CEPO). The convoy was on its way to verify the systematic violations of R-ARCSS and attacks on civilians by the government troops. However, when confronted with evidence of violations, the SSPDF claimed that they were targeting the troops that did not sign the R-ARCSS. The claims were dismissed by the opposition party because all the areas around Wau and Raja were controlled by the opposition force, under the umbrella of the SPLM/A-IO, which signed the peace agreement.

- On 29 October 2018, the South Sudan People's Defence Forces (SSPDF), based in Wadhalelo, allegedly attacked Mabiu, an area under the control of the WBGLF, killing two civilians.

- In their attempts to recapture their previously held positions, on 30 October 2018 the opposition forces ambushed the SSPDF in the area close to Ngo Ku and Ngissa, and they further attacked the government forces based in Wadhalelo.

- On 4 November 2018, clashes persisted in greater Baggari as SSPDF soldiers allegedly launched extensive attacks on surrounding villages, including Ngo Alima.

- The last attack by the government forces on the positions of WBGLF was on 6 November 2018 in Ngo Sulugo area. The government forces were moved from Ngo Baggari to attack civilians in Ngo Sulugo, where they burnt houses and destroyed crops. However, the WBGLF repulsed the attacks and forced the government forces to retreat.

- Although the security arrangement stipulated that all the forces should disengage and be cantoned, the government forces remained scattered around Raja and Wau, in clear violation of both the ACOH and the R-ARCSS.

As Jieng elites had planned before, the constant violence by the government troops led to continued displacement and the steady depopulation of the Fertit and Luo communities from the areas around Wau.

Inside the city, most of Wau's population, predominantly Fertit and Luo, became internally displaced persons (IDPs) and remained inside the United Nations Mission in South Sudan's Protection of Civilians PoC site, as well as in churches. However, the Fertit IDPs also took refuge outside the town, in areas the opposition controlled.

As of February 2019, many men and youths still felt it was too unsafe to leave the PoC site for fear of being targeted. In the evening, streams of people returned from town after visiting their houses because they were still too scared to sleep at home.

The Intergovernmental Authority on Development

The Intergovernmental Authority on Development (IGAD) was biased from day one regarding the High-Level Revitalisation Forum (HLRF) of the Agreement on the Resolution of Conflict in the Republic of South Sudan (ARCSS). The IGAD showed in the coercive language towards the opposition while patting the government on the back. The IGAD Council of Ministers endorsed the preforum consultations report submitted by Dr Ismail Wais in a meeting at the sideline of the AU-EU partnership summit in Abidjan, Côte D'Ivoire, on 28 November 2017. The preforum consultations report was supposed to be the basis for the peace negotiations because it contained the views of all the stakeholders.

But some controversial steps by the Intergovernmental Authority on Development (IGAD) dominated the discussions amongst the ordinary South Sudanese people. Many described the IGAD as a biased and weak organisation that leaned to the government positions. During the peace negotiation, the IGAD actions were heavily in favour of the government's position. For instance, the IGAD refusing to allow renegotiation of ARCSS 2015, which was the government's position, cast doubt on the success of realising genuine peace that could bring real reform.

The president's creation of thirty-two states was a clear violation of the ARCSS of 2015. Unfortunately, the IGAD did nothing to stop the government from proceeding with the new states. The silence of the IGAD encouraged the regime in Juba to commit more violations, which led to war breaking out in July 2016. While the leaders of the SPLM/A-IO were hotly pursued and bombarded by helicopter gunships to the border with the Democratic Republic of Congo (DRC), the members of the IGAD kept demanding they return to Juba and resume their duties in the TGoNU. The government made serious attempts to eliminate senior members of the SPLM/A-IO. The culprit's action was never in doubt, but the IGAD avoided condemning it, which raised questions about the credibility and integrity of the entire organisation.

In July 2018, while the peace talks were underway in Khartoum, President Salva Kiir extended his term in office for a further three years. It was a repetition of the unconstitutional extension of his tenure in office in July 2015. The international community condemned the illegal move by Juba, but the IGAD kept silent on both occasions.

Finally, the IGAD was exposed as a biased peace broker when it employed coercion and intimidation, and it even forced the opposition to append their signatures to an agreement under duress. Many South Sudanese politicians would have preferred a peace mediator other than the IGAD due to a conflict of interest. The majority of IGAD member states had vested interests in South Sudan and would do whatever in their capacity to maintain the status quo.

Oil Revenues

As the government continued to violate the agreement, the international community maintained its position and chose a wait-and-see position. The international community did not fulfil its financial obligations and was rather waiting for the government to carry out its financial obligations; further, the international community waited to see whether the agreement would hold. Most important, they were waiting for the parties to the agreement (both the government and various opposition parties) to show their political will and seriously implement the agreement.

During the peace negotiation in Addis Ababa, the international community demanded the government use oil revenue to fully fund the implementation of the agreement. Unfortunately, the government of South Sudan continued to run the oil sector without transparency, and information about oil revenue remained unclear to the public. The oil continued to run under corrupt management. The way the government managed public resources such as oil was questionable.

First, from the beginning, the government of South Sudan had mortgaged a lot of future oil production by borrowing money from oil companies. It was unclear whether the creditors were acquiring part of the crude oil, receiving financial transaction, or both.

Second, on 26 June 2018, the Republic of South Sudan and the Sudan signed the Khartoum Declaration of Agreement to increase oil production at the Paloch oil field from 127,000 to 180,000 barrels per day. This agreement was not clear to the public in terms of South Sudan's financial commitment with Khartoum. The Khartoum Declaration of Agreement was not clear about how much the South Sudan would compensate the Sudan for pumping the oil to market, as well as any other charges that the Sudanese may impose.

Third, a greater percentage of oil revenue in the South Sudan was either being used for military expenditure or being stolen by the political and military elite.

At the end of 2017, South Sudan produced more than 135,000 barrels per day of oil, and this number trebled at the end of 2018.

Unfortunately, the oil revenue from the government's oil company, Nile Petroleum Corporation Nilepet, was directed to fund Jieng militia responsible for horrific acts of violence in the country. Also, millions of dollars from oil money were paid to several companies partially owned by the family members of top political and military elites responsible for funding the government's militia and military commanders.

Instead of using oil revenue to pay for the public sectors, build infrastructure, and fund the implementation of the R-ARCSS, the government continued to spend oil money on new recruits for the Jieng militia, which was a violation of the R-ARCSS. The state-owned company Nilepet provided support to them via oil money, fuel, military equipment, stipends, food and supplies, and airtime for satellite phones. These Jieng militia continued to be responsible for atrocities, human rights violations, and abuses in the country.

CHAPTER 5

Violation on the Implementation Matrix

During the pretransitional period of the Revitalised Agreement on the Resolution of the Conflict in Republic of South Sudan (R-ARCSS), there were several constraints were facing the implementation matrix, and some of them were artificially made by the government. Some of the serious challenges that faced the implementation matrix were lack of political will and the holdout groups (including the National Salvation Front NAS) that refused to sign the agreement. The obstacles which led to the R-ARCSS's implementation during the pretransitional period proved to be unsuccessful.

A lack of financial support facing the successful implementation of the tasks during the pretransitional period was just a claim and tactic by the government in order to delay some important provisions of the R-ARCSS which were against the interests of the ruling elites.

The lack of political will was because most of the elites and influential senior political and military leaders in the country, who were predominantly members of the Jieng, were exercising the policy of procrastination on the implementation matrix. If implemented, the R-ARCSS would bring democracy, rule of law, accountability, and federalism in the country. The swift implementation of the R-ARCSS would further resolve the issue of controversial states. The R-ARCSS was about the reform issues, which the elites, particularly in the government, disliked. The ruling elites wanted to maintain the status quo in the country and continue with their corruption and tribal agenda in order to finalise their plan. Therefore, they strengthened their military, political, and economic dominance in order to enrich themselves.

The government lacked seriousness about the implementation of most paragraphs in the agreement, especially on the issue of the security arrangements and the number of states in the country. The ruling elites deliberately delayed some important articles of the R-ARCSS, claiming that a lack of funds was to blame. That led the South Sudanese to wonder where the oil revenue was.

Some issues did not need financial support to be implemented, and the government would have addressed them if they had been serious about implementing the R-ARCSS. The issues that did not need to be financed but remained unsolved included the state of emergency since 16 December 2013, despite the peace accord. The ban on opposition parties, some political detainees and prisoners of war remaining in custody of the National Security Services, and other issues could have been addressed positively if the government had been serious about bringing genuine peace to the country.

The lack of financial support from the international community let the government justify the delay in implementation of some articles, such as the issue related to the number of states and the training of opposition forces. In fact, the government was simply denying funding to implement some provisions of the agreement that ruling elites thought would benefit the South Sudanese people, which would be against their plan to dominate and occupy others' lands. For example, the issues of the number of states, if addressed, meant the Fertit would regain their land and Raja would be a separate state from Aweil.

The government, under leadership of President Salva Kiir Mayardit, was quick to demand implementation of other issues which were to the ruling elite's advantage. For example, the government was pushing for the first cantonment of the opposition forces to be in the Panyume and Ngalunga in western and central Equatoria, respectively. By opening the first cantonment areas in these two places, the ruling elites would join their forces with the SPLM/A-IO in order to attack the forces of National Salvation Front (NAS), an opposition under the umbrella of the SSOA—the only opposition that had declined to sign the R-ARCSS. Something that the leadership of the SPLM/A-IO refused.

Also, the government demanded the opposition leaders open the roads and then come to visit the areas controlled by the government and celebrate the peace agreement. The request aimed to convince the international community and the guarantors that they were implementing the peace agreement, therefore attracting them to make a financial contribution. For the ruling elite, the move was also aimed to create a situation whereby the country would look like it normalised, but they were not really implementing the agreement.

As of February 2019, most of the activities that were supposed to be implemented in the implementation matrix required by R-ARCSS were not realised as stipulated in the agreement. Concerning the formation of the committees that should have been responsible for the implementation of the R-ARCSS, although some of these Committees have been formed, most of them were not operating or had not even conducted their regular meetings according to the implementation matrix in order to for them to carry out their duties as stipulated in the agreement.

Below are outlined notices that had been made concerning the formation and the activities of these committees during the pretransitional period.

National Pre-Transitional Committee NPTC

Although the National Pre-Transitional Committee (NPTC) was not formed within two weeks as stipulated in the R-ARCSS, fortunately the committee was established. However, this important committee has not fulfilled its mandate tasks demanded by the R-ARCSS in Sub-Article 1.4.7.3, per the agreement.

The NPTC has been assigned to draw a roadmap for implementing the political tasks of the pretransitional period, as well as prepare a budget for the activities during the pretransitional period. According to the R-ARCSS, within three to five weeks after 12 September 2018, which was the date the R-ARCSS was signed, the NPTC should have put in place the timeline for implementing the political tasks during the pretransitional period. Unfortunately, the NPTC failed to do so.

Instead of pushing for the implementation of the R-ARCSS, by funding the activities of the pretransitional period, in its early stage the members of the NPTC quickly involved in mass corruption without the knowledge of members of the opposition parties in the NPTC. The corruption was represented by issuing fake contracts with unregistered companies in order to mismanage public resources. Examples of these contracts were the order of a huge amount of money, in millions of US dollars, to renovate the houses of some politicians, including the house of Vice President Taban Deng Gai.

Also, on 5 November 2018, Tut Gatluak, the presidential advisor on security, and the chairperson of the NPTC issued an order from the office of the president requesting the secretary of the NPTC finalise a contract where the NPTC paid US$94,505,000 to the company, which was faked to have the name of Green for Logistics Services. According to the contract, the company would supply one thousand vehicles to the government elites in the capital, Juba, and in Bahr el Ghazal.

The fake company, Green Logistic Services, claimed to have issued a confirmation letter to the NPTC informing them that they had delivered 500 Toyota Land Cruisers (LC V8 model) worth $60 million, or $120,000 for each car; 200 Toyota Hilux for $11 million, or $55,000 for each car; and 150 Hardtops equal to about $11.8 million, or about $78,700 for each car.

Unfortunately, no house was renovated, and no cars were delivered. Even the original price of the Toyota Land Cruiser, LC V8 model, was less than what was in the contract. The real price of the LC V8 model was worth $58,000.

Further, because the NPTC was supposed to carry out its duties, the NPTC should issue a monthly written report on the implementation of R-ARCSS. However, the committee failed to submit any report to the R-JMEC, chairpersons of the parties, and other stakeholders as required by the agreement under Article 1.4.7.4.

One of the important steps to the agreement was required funding for the implementation of the R-ARCSS during the pretransitional period. In this regard, the government was required to contribute financially in order to support the implementation of the agreement. The international community made its contribution contingent on the demonstration of political will by the parties to implement R-ARCSS, including the government delivering on its financial commitment.

After a long delay, the government made an announcement of $280 million US as the budget for the implementation of the agreement during the pretransitional period. During the negotiation of the agreement, the parties agreed on relocation of the oil income to fund the implementation. Unfortunately, the establishment of the fund for the implementation of R-ARCSS was delayed until 23 January 2019, when the government tactically announced that it had transferred only around $1.4 million into the account of the National Pre-Transitional Committee for implementing activities during the pretransitional period. The government should have established the fund and contributed at least half of the budget immediately after 12 September 2018, as required by the agreement under Article 1.4.8. As a result of the delay, no funding was secured from the international community, and most of the articles stipulated by the R-ARCSS were never implemented or delayed.

Independent Boundaries Commission

After the country was divided into controversial states by the presidential decree, many communities' lands were annexed to the Jieng. The majority of the non-Jieng in the Republic of the South Sudan considered the creation of the new states as occupation of their lands. The move prompted strong disagreement amongst the South Sudanese communities on the newly created, controversial states by the president. The annexation of non-Jieng land by the president fuelled unrest between the members of the government (predominantly Jieng elites) and the different ethnic groups in the country.

Although the majority of the South Sudanese people rejected the structure of the new states, the government continued to forcefully proceed with the implementation of the new states. Therefore during the peace negotiation, the creation of the Independent Boundaries Commission (IBC) and the Technical Boundaries Commission (TBC) was decided and given a mandate to resolve the issue of the number of states in the country, with the condition that the IBC and the TBC must complete their tasks within the pretransitional period. According to the R-ARCSS in Article

1.15.1, the IGAD executive secretariat was required to form the IBC within two weeks after 12 September 2018.

Even though the formation of the TBC was not within seven days from 12 September 2018 as stipulated in the R-ARCSS, Sub-Article 1.15.18.1, the TBC failed to conclude its tasks within sixty days, as stipulated in the agreement.

Resolving the issue of the states would be against the interests of the Jieng elites, and therefore the government was not interested in forming and funding the IBC and TBC. However, as of February 2019, the tasks given to both committees had not fulfilled. The lack of resolving the controversial issue of the thirty-two states before the beginning of the transitional period will probably lead to another unsustainable peace in the country.

National Constitutional Amendment Committee (NCAC)

Per the agreement, the National Constitutional Amendment Committee was supposed to be formed in order to incorporate the R-ARCSS into the Transitional Constitution of South Sudan (TCSS) of 2011, as amended. The incorporation should be completed within twenty-one days from 12 September 2018, as stipulated in Article 1.18.1.1. Although the NCAC had been established by the agreement, as of February 2019, the committee has fallen short of drafting the Constitutional Amendment Bill by incorporating the R-ARCSS into the Transitional Consitution of South Sudan (TCSS) within the required term. Further, the government resisted the idea of a federalism phrase, which was to be incorporated into the TCRSS.

Cessation of Hostilities

According to the Agreement of Cessation of Hostilities, Protection of Civilians and Humanitarian (ACOH) and the R-ARCSS, under Articles 2.1.4 and 2.1.5, respectively, the parties to the agreement should demonstrate a permanent ceasefire, disengage and separate their forces, withdraw foreign troops, report in advance any of their potential movement of forces, and open corridors to humanitarian organisations. Unfortunately, although the SPLM/A-IO made its commitment, the government failed to follow through.

Also, all parties were supposed to cease new recruitment of security forces and training of new recruits, as stipulated in Article 2.1.8. This was violated by the government. The government continued to recruit and train new private militia in many places. Examples of the training of new recruits by the government were in Luri, Warrap, and Twic.

In the Luri area, where there was a government military base, a team of Ceasefire and Transitional Security Arrangements Monitoring Mechanism (CTSAMVM) suspected the area was in violation and went to verify. Unfortunately, the team of international monitors was prevented from entering the training area. The South Sudanese security personals then detained, stripped, blindfolded, and assaulted three international observers and one South Sudanese driver in the Luri area, in the western parts of Juba, on 18 December 2018.

The government assigned Major General Makiir Gai to transfer a huge number of weapons and food items to Warrap State, where they opened military training bases for private militia. The director of National Security Services, General Akol Koor, and one of the commanders of Tiger Forces, Lual Wek, were assigned by the president to supervise the new recruitment process.

The government security forces forcefully approached the ordinary Jieng household in Warrap and the surrounding areas, ordering them to contribute one cow and one male adult to the new recruits. The forceful recruitment of Jieng youths faced resistance from ordinary Jieng, who chose to support the peace agreement.

Also, the local government in Twic State, a predominant Jieng state, sought massive, forceful recruitment of Jieng youths, which led to intellectual Jiengs from the state to issue a letter of protest against the massive recruitment of their youths on 26 January 2019. The letter was directed to the government and the IGAD office.

During the peace negotiation, because it was an important issue, the matter of cantonment of forces took a long time to be negotiated and finalised. Although it was difficult to reach an agreement, finally the parties agreed on a formula by which all armed forces were to be cantoned and later unified, in order to create a nucleus national army for South Sudan.

The pretransitional period was chosen to be eight months as a result of the time needed to assemble and train all forces jointly, so as to be deployed before the return of opposition leaders to the capital. The created national army should then provide reliable security to all parties, especially the opposition leaders, and avoid any repeated military confrontations, such as in 2016, which caused the breakdown of ARCSS and the renewal of civil war in the country.

The Ceasefire and Transitional Security Arrangements Monitoring Mechanism (CTSAMVM) was given a mandate to implement the security arrangements in the country. However, the CTSAMVM was continuously denied access by the government and could not even visit any location of the government forces in order to ascertain the information given to them. Also, the government tactically delayed the process of cantonment of the opposition forces. The cantonment of forces failed to be completed within thirty days from 12 September 2018, as agreed to under Articles 2.2.2 and 2.2.3.3.

Prisoners of War

According to both the ACOH and the R-ARCSS, all POWs and political detainees were supposed to be immediately released and handed over to the International Committee of the Red Cross (ICRC) as stipulated in both agreements, particularly in the R-ARCSS under Article 2.1.6. Immediately after the signing of the ACOH, the opposition parties released those government affiliates who were considered to be POWs, including those under WBGLF detention around Raja and Wau.

Unfortunately, only after pressure from the international community did the government release some POWs and political detainees, and the procedure of their release was not according to Article 2.1.6. The agreement under Article 2.1.6 called for releasing the prisoners through the ICRC. A number of POWs and political detainees were still under government detention. This was a serious violation, which indicated that despite the damages that the senior members of the ruling party caused to the country, the ruling elites were not willing to reconcile with the people of the South

Sudan. It also indicated a lack of political will, because the ruling elites sought their own interests.

Following the implementation matrix according to the R-ARCSS, the activities involving the demilitarisation of civilian centres and the collection of long- and medium-range heavy weapons were supposed to be completed within forty-five days from 12 September 2018, as stipulated in Sub-Articles 2.2.3.1 and 2.2.3.2. However, civilian properties, especially in the WBG region, were still occupied by the government troops. The government forces, the SSPDF, still were not cantoned, especially in the WBG region. This violation also indicated that the government was unwilling to implement the security arrangements.

Joint Transitional Security Committee (JTSC)

Under the article of R-ARCSS, within fifteen days the Joint Transitional Security Committee was supposed to set the eligibility criteria for candidates willing to serve in the unified national army, the National Security Service (NSS), police, prisons, fire brigade, and wildlife services. Also, the agreement further mandated that the JTSC plan and execute the unification of all forces, as stipulated in Article 2.2.8.

Unfortunately, the time frame for conducting these activities passed. The government officials were unwilling to proceed and fund the cantonment of the opposition army. The government interpreted the cantonment of the opposition army as a way to modernise, train, and upgrade the opposition forces to be equal to the government forces. Therefore it was not in the interests of their plan to dominate the South Sudan's future national army.

The failure of the JTSC to carry out its mandate led to the parties in the agreement to fail to commence the joint training of the necessary unified forces of the military, police, and other security services, as stipulated by the R-ARCSS under Article 2.2.9.

Disarmament, Demobilisation, and Reintegration Commission (DDRC)

According to the R-ARCSS, within 30 days from 12 September 2018, which is the day the party signed the agreement, there should be establishment of Disarmament, Demobilisation and Reintegration

Commission DDRC. Unfortunately, the parties failed to reconstitute the DDRC, as was stipulated in the agreement under Article 2.4.9. This affected other activities related to the commission during the pretransitional period.

All the above-mentioned constraints and delays were deliberate and artificial obstacles made by the ruling elite in order to make it difficult for the peace implementation. This allowed them to continue with their political and economic dominance in the country. The Jieng political and military leaders wanted to continue with their plan of occupying other communities' lands.

CHAPTER 6

CONCLUSION

The emergence of the Fertit revolution against the government and the policy of the Jieng Council of Elders was a result of the Jieng elite's dominance, marginalisation, violation, and aggression against the Fertit. Therefore the Fertit desired self-determination and sought a resolution to define their own economic and political status, maintain their identity, and have control over their own land and people in the face of being marginalised by military and political elites from the Jieng tribe. These struggles have originated from causes in the past, dating back to the independence of Sudan. The Fertit ethnic groups' decision to wage the struggle were reinforced by several events, particularly the attempts by the Jieng to force the Fertit to emigrate from their land in 2012, the violation of Fertit rights, and the annexation of Fertit land by the creation of controversial new states in the Republic of South Sudan.

Fertit has long been demanding the following.

1. A federal system of governance in the Republic of South Sudan, by creating federal states' own executive, legislative, judicial, and security apparatus. The Fertit leaders introduced this demand during the Torit Mutiny in 1955.
2. Wau and Raja, or a whole WGB region, should be a separate and independent state, with its borders as they stood on 1 January 1956.
3. The soil of Wau State should consist of six areas: Baggari, Bisselia, Kpaile, Kuajiena, Marial Baii, Udici, and Wau County. Wau

should be both a county and a municipality of Wau State. The soil of Raja State should consist of Raja, Ringi, Timsah, Kafia Kingi, Sopo, Boro, Dulo, and Uyujuku City.

4. Cattle grazing in the WBG region should be restricted, organised, and regulated by the local governments in order to avoid the destruction of agricultural farms.

5. All the lands which have been illegally distributed to the government officials, especially to noncitizens of the WBG region, should be returned.

6. The indigenous ethnic groups of the WBG region should take the lead in any allocation of public posts and local business opportunities.

7. The indigenous tribes of the WBG region should be represented at the national level, particularly in the National Executive Council, the National Legislative Assembly, commissions, embassies, and other central institutions.

Fertit ethnic groups were not alone in refusing Jieng domination; other communities in the Republic of South Sudan are on the same page. The Shilluk in Upper Nile, to the west, have had a similar revolution against the takeover of their kingdom by the Padang, a Jieng subtribe. The Equatorians to the south have demanded federalism for decades, for similar reasons.

Developments since the independence of the Sudan, the period after the Addis Ababa Agreement in 1970s, the formation of the SPLM/A, and the beginning of Sudanese Civil War in the 1980s, leading to the independent of the South Sudan, have solidified the conviction amongst Fertit political and military leaders that they were and continue to be vulnerable to political and economic marginalisation and genocide, unless they physically fight for their own rights and survival. It is these beliefs that will probably continue fuelling conflict in the WBG region in particular and the Republic of South Sudan in general.

After illustrating the causes of Fertit insurgence, it was also important to explore the crucial question of how a culturally peace-loving community, the Fertit tribe, adapted to the hard new reality forced on their shoulders. They decided to respond by organising their opposition in order to protect themselves from aggression. In fact, for the second time, the Fertit community did not voluntarily choose to establish their own forces to protect themselves; they were pushed to do so.

As explained earlier, the first event that prompted the beginning of tension between the two communities was the Torit Mutiny. The second event was when the SPLA soldiers, predominantly from the Jieng tribe, violently attacked Fertit neighbourhoods in 1980s; this was considered the beginning of serious threats by the Jieng against the Fertit community. The Fertit ethnic groups managed to counter the aggression, and they survived an attempted genocide.

The last event was a result of the second one. After independence of the country, the leadership of the SPLM/A became a higher political and military authority in the country. They captured this opportunity to orchestrate revenge attacks against the Fertit community. This period was characterised by government forces and the Mathiang Anyor violent attacking, abusing, and destroying Fertit property.

The formation of an alliance between the Fertit opposition forces and the SPLM/A-IO was on rocky ground. The Fertit leaders' allegiance was based on the belief that the local grievances that inspired them to establish their opposition could be resolved at the national level. Further, Fertit leaders came to know that it was in their best interest to participate in reforming the whole country through participation on the national level, not only in the WBG region. In 2014 the SPLM/A-IO under Riek Machar was the only national platform available that offered this opportunity. The SPLM/A-IO began as a national reform movement and demanded federalism, rule of law, democracy, and accountability. These issues were Fertit concerns as well. The Fertit leaders would continue to be strong allies to the SPLM/A-IO as long as the leadership of the SPLM/A-IO embraced the same issues.

Discontinuing the Fertit insurgency and successfully ending the fighting in the WBG region in the future will depend on the government addressing the roots of the conflicts in the region and in the country as a whole. If, in contrast, key demands on issues that have caused the conflict are not addressed, it is likely that the armed struggle will continue, particularly for the Fertit ethnic groups.

Final Thoughts

Throughout the existence of the Western Bahr el Ghazal region, the region has gone through tensions and conflicts, and ethnic animosity amongst the WBG community, especially the Jieng and Fertit, has increased. After South Sudan's independence in 2011, moreover, the ethnic animosity has deepened further due to the tragic shooting of peaceful protestors in December 2012. Thousands of Fertit civilians have known hardly anything but war. Unfortunately, war became part of their lives and the lives of many ethnicities in the country. South Sudan has become a militarised society.

Regrettably, the political and military leaders in the ruling party, the SPLM/A, often have ethnic power bases, creating an ethnic dimension to most conflicts in the country. The reality that South Sudanese society has to face is that the ethnic conflicts have deepened the ethnic animosity within one group. For instance, all ethnicities in the South Sudan have divided their own groups into two to fight either with the government troops or one of the opposition parties. As an example, there are some members of the Nuer ethnicity who remain with the government troops to fight the SPLA IO, which are predominantly Nuer.

Fortunately, although there are tens of thousands who have been killed during the conflict, in Fertit society a culture of revenge is not prominent. The region has strong traditions of peace making and reconciliation, often through the chiefs or the churches. The political leaders' best efforts will be needed if a lasting peace is to be achieved. All sides have to call for forgiveness, reconciliation, and peaceful coexistence.

Peace Implementation

Until recently, the international community focused its attention on the negotiation of peace agreements to resolve conflicts in the Republic of South Sudan, and it paid little attention to an effective implementation process. Unfortunately, the last five years have proven that insufficiency in implementation of agreements has led to serious consequences, such as a failure to achieve sustainable peace in the country. The notion that an agreement between the regime in Juba and armed opposition parties would remain binding in the postagreement phase has been dishonest.

Reality reveals that in the 1980s and 1990s, the just, negotiated agreements in such countries as Angola, Cambodia, and Liberia collapsed and resulted into new, deadly violence. In some cases, more blood was shed after the failure to implement a peace accord. This was a reality in the Republic of South Sudan in 2016, when the government dishonoured the ARCSS, and the result was the widening of the conflict.

Moreover, after the successful implementation of the Comprehensive Peace Agreement CPA of 9 January 2005, the government, under the leadership of President Salva Kiir Mayardit, was blamed for failing to implement most of the agreements the government had with the opposition parties. Even when a settlement was negotiated and agreed upon, such as the ARCSS of August 2015, a simplistic and a short-term view of how to implement it led the government to undermine the successful implementation of the agreement in the Republic of South Sudan.

That resulted in the majority of the South Sudanese people to continuously feel sceptical and suspicious of implementing any future agreements, specifically the R-ARCSS. Some of the factors that led to a failure to implement peace agreements in the country continue to be lack of political will to implement an agreement from the elites in Juba; security dilemmas amongst the warring parties; inadequate international community involvement; the presence of spoilers whose commitment to peace is only tactical; vague, incomplete, or expedient peace agreements; and the lack of coordination amongst implementing agencies. Such elements are merely a first step to understanding the problem of implementation in the country.

The government of the South Sudan, which is predominantly Jieng senior military and political leaders and which has been associated with the leadership of President Salva Kiir Mayardit, continuously assumes (incorrectly) that the government can achieve peace and therefore stabilise the economy through military victory. Unfortunately, the Jieng elites have not discovered from past conflicts that even if they succeeded, winning the war militarily would not bring a sustainable peace in the Republic of South

Sudan. Peaceful resolution and effective implementation of an agreement remain fundamental aspects of resolving the conflicts in the country.

Moreover, additional critical factors of successful peace implementation in the Republic of South Sudan are demobilisation, disarmament of civilians armed by the Juba regime, restructuring of armed forces to be a national army, political will, and reconciliation amongst the leaders. The absence of these factors allows for a lack of implementation of any agreement and a continuation of conflict in the Republic of South Sudan.

Recommendation

Security Arrangement

In future security arrangements, the cities, particularly the capital of Juba, should be strictly demilitarised. There should not be any unified forces deployed inside cities, as stipulated in the R-ARCSS, to protect the political leaders. The protection of all political leaders should be assigned to small groups of VIP Protection Guards, each of which serves a specific leader. These VIP protection units should be designed to deny each elite a leverage of implying threats.

Federalism

It is no secret that ethnic violence exists in the Republic of South Sudan. Ethnic violence also exists in different parts of the world—for example, in the former Yugoslavia, Burundi, Tamil, and Burma. The former Yugoslavia had diversely different societies, and all its previous governments attempted to bring the different populations into a peaceful coexistence, but they failed because of the system of governance. Violence eventually broke out, and the country disintegrated.

In other countries where there is also ethnic diversity, they have put in place a system that encourages peaceful coexistence. An example is Switzerland, which has a diverse ethnic population with different religions and linguistic backgrounds. These issues continue to be the cause of ethnic conflicts in other places in the world, especially in the Republic of South Sudan.

How did Switzerland achieve a successful peaceful coexistence amongst its diverse population when others failed? In order to live in peace, Switzerland's multidimensional subpopulations are separated by both political and physical borders. There are political borders in the form of a federal system of governance, and there are physical boundaries formed by the country's natural border of mountains and lakes.

The idea that local autonomy is a good way to organise a government is present in other places, such as the United States of America, which has municipal, district, state, and federal government systems. This model of governance absolutely fit the Republic of South Sudan, but unfortunately it was not implemented because Jieng elites found it difficult to dominate others under the federal system. Domination remains amongst the causes of ethnic conflict in the world, particularly in the South Sudan, where national governments have had the most governing authority since the creation of the country.

The country is inhabited by more than sixty-four different ethnic groups, so a federal system of governance is the only system that can reduce ethnic tension and prevent future violence amongst the ethnic groups. Self-governance at the state and municipal (or district) level is the only system that can offer all South Sudan ethnic groups a sense of autonomy and safety.

Given the scale of destruction, death, and suffering caused by ethnic violence in the country, South Sudanese political leaders have to identify and develop a political system where their different ethnic groups can live in peace. Rather than forcing them to become integrated, they can provide for peaceful coexistence by introducing a political system that suits them. The South Sudanese's natural tendency to self-aggregate can be leveraged for peace if the people of South Sudan are given proper borders and self-governance over their own lands.

In a separate development, the National Dialogue Committee, established by the president, held a regional dialogue conference from 25 February 2019 to 2 March 2019 in Wau. The Bahr el Ghazal citizens opposed the current decentralised form of governance, where the national government has controls over states. Instead, the vast majority of the people of Bahr el Ghazal region (including Jieng) demanded the implementation of federalism as the system of governance in South Sudan.

The National Dialogue Committee is the brainchild of President Salva Kiir and the Jieng Council of Elders, who are opposed to federalism. Hence, the massive support for federalism in Bahr Ghazal is a big blow to the ruling elites. It's confirmation that federalism remains popular across South Sudan.

The South Sudanese are not about to be cowed into submission by the tribal government. The South Sudanese people are resolute in their struggle to bring about a federal system of governance that will give power to the people and local states. They will continue to be steadfast in their quest to realise a just peace and a real democracy. They will not accept a fake one under coercion and intimidation.

REFERENCES

Africa Watch. *Denying the Honour of Living* (New York: Africa Watch, 1990).

African Union Commission of Inquiry on South Sudan AUCISS. "Final Report of the African Union Commission of Inquiry on South Sudan". AU Peace and Security Commission, 15 October 2014.

Africans Press. "S. Sudan Governor Faints after Brother Killed in Clashes with Rebels", 13 April 2017.

Al Jazeera. "South Sudan President Signs Peace Deal with Rebels", 27 August 2015.

Al Jazeera. "South Sudan Ceasefire Violated Hours after Taking Effect", 30 June 2018.

Ali, Ali Abdel Gadir, Ibrahim A. Elbadawi, and Atta el-Batahani. "Sudan's Civil War: Why Has It Prevailed for So Long?", in Paul Collier and Nicholas Sambanis, eds., *Understanding Civil War: Evidence and Analysis* (Washington, DC: World Bank, 2005), 193–220.

Amnesty International. "South Sudan: Civil Unrest and State Repression: Human Rights Violations in Wau, WBG State", 2013.

Baas, Saskia. *From Civilians to Soldiers and from Soldiers to Civilians: Mobilisation and Demobilisation in Sudan* (Amsterdam: Amsterdam University Press, 2012).

Badal, Raphael K. "Political Cleavages within the Southern Sudan: An Empirical Analysis of the Redivision Debate", in Sharif Harir and Terje Tvedt, eds., *Short-cut to Decay: The Case of the Sudan* (Uppsala: Nordic Africa Institute, 1994), 104–124.

Berkeley, B. "Sounds of Violence: Rwanda's Killer Radio", *New Republic* 21/8–9 (1994), 18–19.

Blocq, Daniel S. "The Grassroots Nature of Counterinsurgent Tribal Militia Formation: The Case of the Fertit in Southern Sudan, 1985–1989", *Journal of Eastern African Studies*. 8/4 (2014), 710–724.

Borst, B. "Burundi-media: Journalists Combat Influence of 'Hate Media'", Inter Press Service (9 August 1995).

Camp Coordination and Camp Management CCCM. "CCCM Cluster Bi-weekly Situation Report", Humanitarian Response (14 June 2018).

Carey, Sabine C., Michael Colaresi, and Neil Mitchell. "Why Do Governments Use Militias?" Paper presented at conference, "Paramilitaries, Militias and Civil Defence Forces in Civil Wars", Yale University, October 2012.

Carey, Sabine C., Neil J. Mitchell, and Will Lowe. "States, the Security Sector, and the Monopoly of Violence: A New Database on Pro-government Militias", *Journal of Peace Research* 50/2 (2013), 249–258. doi: 10.1177/0022343312464881.

Cavell, Anna. "Protesters Shot at by South Sudanese Army", Al Jazeera (16 December 2012).

Collins, Robert O. *Shadows in the Grass: Britain in the Southern Sudan 1918–1956* (New Haven, CT: Yale University Press, 1983).

Collins, Robert O. *The Southern Sudan, 1883–1898: A Struggle for Control* (New Haven, CT: Yale University Press, 1962).

Collins, Robert O. *The Southern Sudan in Historical Perspective* (Tel Aviv: University of Tel Aviv, 1975).

Daly, M. W. *Empire on the Nile: The Anglo-Egyptian Sudan 1898–1934* (Cambridge: Cambridge University Press, 1986).

Daly, M. W. *Imperial Sudan: The Anglo-Egyptian Condominium, 1934–56* (Cambridge: Cambridge University Press, 1991).

Douglas H. Johnson. "Brief Analysis of the Boundaries of the 28 States", Brief Analysis of 28 States Boundaries for Centre for Peace and Development Studies. University of Juba.

Dinka Development Plan for 200 Years. "The Jieng Council of Elders (JCE) 2015 Master Plan", http://www.southsudannation.com/the-jieng-council-of-elders-jce-2015-master-plan-dinka-development-plan-for-200-years, accessed March 2017.

Green city Media. "S. Sudan President Salva Kiir's Speech from Wau: Need for Peaceful Coexistence between Dinka and Fertit", Mixcloud (2012).

Government of the Republic of South Sudan. Local Government Act. 1 January 2009.

Government of the Republic of South Sudan. Establishment Order 36/2015. 2 October 2015.

Government of the Republic of South Sudan. Establishment Order 1/2017. 14 January 2017.

Government of the Republic of South Sudan, Commission of Inquiry. "Report of the Investigation Committee on Wau Incident of 24th–26th June 2016." 1 August 2016.

Gray, Richard. *A History of the Southern Sudan: 1839–1889* (Oxford: Oxford University Press, 1961).

Gurtong. "Fertit, Luo and Dinka Marial Baii of Bahr el Ghazal Reconciliation Conference in Khartoum", 27 June 2005.

Harir, Sharif, and Terje Tvedt, eds. *Short-cut to Decay: The Case of the Sudan* (Uppsala: Nordic Africa Institute, 1994).

Human Rights Watch. "South Sudan: Civilians Killed, Tortured in Western Region: Provide Justice for Army Abuses in Western Regions", 24 May 2016.

Human Rights Watch. "South Sudan: Events of 2016", in World Report 2017.

Human Rights Watch. "South Sudan: No Justice for Protester Killings: Full and Impartial Investigations Needed for Wau Deaths", 24 May 2013.

Intergovernmental Authority on Development. "Agreement on the Resolution of the Conflict in the Republic of South Sudan", 17 August 2015.

Intergovernmental Authority on Development. "Revitalised Agreement on the Resolution of the Conflict in the Republic of South Sudan (R-ARCSS)", Addis Ababa, 12 September 2018.

Kellow, Christine L., and H. Leslie Steeves. "The Role of Radio in the Rwandan Genocide", http://media.leeds.ac.uk/papers/pmt/exhibits/2192/Rwandaradio.pdf.

Kurimoto, Eisei. "Civil War and Regional Conflicts: The Pari and Their Neighbours in South-eastern Sudan", in Katsuyoshi Fukui and John Markakis, eds., *Ethnicity and Conflict in the Horn of Africa* (Athens: Ohio University Press, 1994), 95–111.

Minority Rights Group International. "Sudan: Dinka", in *World Directory of Minorities and Indigenous Peoples* (July 2008).

Mire, Lawrence, and John Ralph Willis, eds. *Al-Zubayr Pasha and the Zariba Based Slave Trade in the Bahr al-Ghazal 1855-1879. Slaves and Slavery in Muslim Africa: Vol II, the Servile Estate* (New York: Psychology Press), 117.

Petersen, Roger D. *Understanding Ethnic Violence: Fear, Hatred, Resentment in Twentieth Century Eastern Europe* (New York: Cambridge University Press, 2012).

Pinaud, Clemence. "South Sudan: Civil War, Predation and the Making of a Military Aristocracy", *African Affairs* 113/451 (April 2014), 192–211.

R-ARCSS. https://www.jmecsouthsudan.org/index.php/arcss-2015/igad-hlrf-agreement/108-revitalised-agreement-on-the-resolution-of-the-conflict-in-the-republic-of-south-sudan-r-arcss-2018/file, accessed 12 September 2018.

Rolandsen, Øystein H. "A False Start: Between War and Peace in the Southern Sudan, 1956–62", *Journal of African History* 52/1 (2011), 105–123. doi: 10.1017/S0021853711000107.

Rutherford, A., D. Harmon, J. Werfel, S. Bar-Yam, A. S. Gard-Murray, A. Gros, and Y. Bar-Yam, "Good Fences: The Importance of Setting Boundaries for Peaceful Coexistence", *PLoS ONE* 9/5 (May 21, 2014), e95660. doi: 10.1371/journal.pone.0095660.

Salih, Mohammed. "'New Wine in Old Bottles': Tribal Militias and the Sudanese State", *Review of African Political Economy* 16/45–46 (1989), 168–174. doi: 10.1080/03056248908703838.

Salih, Mohammed, and Sharif Harir. "Tribal Militias: The Genesis of National Disintegration", in Sharif Harir and Terje Tvedt, eds., *Short-cut to Decay: The Case of the Sudan*, 185–202.

Sanderson, Lilian Passmore, and Neville Sanderson. *Education, Religion and Politics in Southern Sudan, 1899–1964* (London: Evergreen Books, 1981).

Santandrea, Stefano. *Ethno-geography of the Bahr el Ghazal (Sudan): An Attempt at a Historical Reconstruction* (Bologna: Editrice Missionaria Italiana, 1981).

The Sentry. "Stopping the Looting and Destruction in South Sudan", https://thesentry.org/wp-content/uploads/2016/08/Sentry_WCSP_Final.pdf, accessed July 2017.

Sikainga, Ahmed A. *Western Bahr al-Ghazal under British Rule, 1898–1956* (Athens: Ohio University Press, 1991).

Stefano Santandrea. "A Popular history of Wau", https://sudanarchive.net/cgi-bin/pagessoa?a=pdf&d=Dnbd1.1.1&dl=1&sim=Screen2Image.

Alex Ryan and Daniel G. Cox. Countering Insurgency and the Myth of "The Cause", ASPJ Africa & Francophonie (4th Quarter 2017). DOI http://dx.doi.org/10.5038/1944-0472.8.1.1419

South Sudan Map. http://www.geographicguide.com/africa-maps/south-sudan.htm, accessed February 2019.

Su, Alice. "Splits and Schisms in South Sudan: How the Creation of More States Is Undermining Peace", IRIN (16 June 2016).

Woodward, Peter. *Sudan, 1898–1989: The Unstable State* (Boulder, CO: Lynne Reinner, 1990).

World Statesmen. "States of the Sudan since 1991", http://www.worldstatesmen.org/Sudan_prov.html, accessed January 2019.

Young, John. "Sudan: Liberation Movements, Regional Armies, Ethnic Militias & Peace", *Review of African Political Economy* 30/97 (2003), 423–434. doi: 10.1080/06.

ABOUT THE AUTHOR

 Dominic Ukelo is a South Sudanese citizen, who joined the opposition party after he saw his own people been slaughtered by the government forces in 2012. Immediately, after the graduation and short period of work, he left his job and travelled through the liberated areas under opposition control, where civilians sought a refuge.

His work, in defending the rights of marginalized voiceless people in the country and raise their demands, has been praised by many.

Before he joined the opposition, he studied a Bachelor of International Business and Administration, in Haaga-Helia University Applied Sciences, Finland 2008-2013.

Studied Master of Banking and Finance, Kingston University of London, the United Kingdom UK 2013-2014

Worked in Santander Bank in London, 2014-2015. And

Worked with the state government of Vantaa, Finland 2016-2017

www.ingramcontent.com/pod-product-compliance
Lightning Source LLC
Chambersburg PA
CBHW031914270726
48655CB00001BA/349